David and Lisa

Jordi

Little Ralphie
and the Creature

David and Lisa

—⚏—

Jordi

—⚏—

Little Ralphie
and the Creature

Theodore Isaac Rubin, M.D.

A Tom Doherty Associates Book

New York

This book is printed on acid-free paper.

The story "David and Lisa" has been previously published with
the title "Lisa and David."

A Forge Book
Published by Tom Doherty Associates, Inc.
175 Fifth Avenue
New York, NY 10010

Forge® is a registered trademark of Tom Doherty Associates, Inc.

Design by Susan Hood

ISBN 0-312-87003-5

First Edition: November 1998

Printed in the United States of America

0 9 8 7 6 5 4 3 2 1

Contents

Author's Note

In the time that has elapsed since the first two stories of this book have been written, the human condition has not changed appreciably.

Despite much progress in electronics, scientific theory, and medicine people continue to have people problems.

We have as many—and even—more people with emotional problems as ever. There are still many Jordis, Lisas, Davids, and Ralphies. There are still people with lesser and greater difficulties. The simple fact remains that none of us are exempt. Stresses and conflicts—both internal and external—and socioeconomic problems and pressures are ever-present. Fortunately, human beings are highly adaptable creatures. But constructive change and healthy adaptation take much more time than mechanical inventions. We continue to struggle to know ourselves and to constructively relate to each other.

Psychogenic drugs have been very helpful in certain conditions. Unfortunately, this does not pertain in all conditions. Sustained relief based on deep personality changes takes time and insight. There is still no substitute for compassionate understanding, caring, kindness, and all that comes under the heading of real love.

T. I. R.

David and Lisa

In memory of Nathan Freeman, M.D.
Teacher and Friend

I want to thank my wife, Ellie, for both inspiration and technical assistance; and my children, Trudy, Jeff, and Eugene for helping me to understand other children.

Preface

This is a love story of two exceptional children.

The place is a residential treatment center.

The time, one year after admission, is a crucial period in their lives during which communication becomes possible.

A big fat sow, a big black cow—and how and how and how.

"A big fat cow, a big black sow—and how and how and how.

"A cow, a cow; a sow, a sow—big and fat, big and fat; so they sat—so they sat, they sat; so they sat."

She hopped around the room, first on one foot, then on the other. On her left foot she always said, "sow," and on her right foot, "cow." She sat down on the floor each time she said, "They sat, they sat." But in seconds she was up again—hopping around the room and, in a loud, clear, high-pitched voice, saying, "A cow, a cow; a sow, a sow—black, black, black, black, black, black, black, black." Her voice changed. She was shrieking now. Then she sat down, held her head with her hands, and moved it up and back, moaning softly. "Dark, dark, dark, dark, dark—so, so, so, so dark."

Fuddy-dud-dud, fuddy-dud-dud-duddy—fud-fud-duddy fud-fud.

"Scudy-rud—rud-scud, rud-scud; duddy-scud fud rud, duddy scud fud rud."

She sat in the corner and repeated the sequence over and over again. John tried to engage her in a sensible conversation—but to no avail. She listened to him, looked at him, and repeated the sequence again and again.

David listened and wondered what she meant. He finally gave up and thought about a big calendar clock he had seen a year ago.

That night before he fell asleep he had a fantasy. The sky was absolutely clear of clouds, the air cool, crisp, and dry. Thousands upon thousands of stars were visible. Planets could be seen, and the sun and moon, too. Beyond it all there were other suns and planets, other universes. They all moved perfectly, precisely, in exact relation to one another. The universes and galaxies and universes beyond them had all become part of a huge mechanism. It was the Universal Time Clock, and it measured Universal Time. He lay back and smiled, for after all he, David Green, was The Universal Timekeeper—or, better yet, Keeper of *the* Time—all Time.

He made sure the cover was tucked about him perfectly. He lay still—and fell asleep, his right hand clutched around the ancient teddy bear ear under his pillow. The light remained on all night.

———

John, John, begone, begone—enough, enough of this stuffy stuff."

"Are you angry with me, Lisa?"

"Angry, angry—bangry, wangry,—be gone, John; John, be gone."

"I guess you are angry. What is it that makes you so angry?"

"You foo, you foo—it's you, it's you—it's you, you foo; foo you, foo you."

She suddenly broke into a wild screaming laugh. She screamed and laughed continuously, imperceptibly inhaling air to laugh some more. After five minutes he interrupted her. "You're still angry, aren't you, Lisa?"

She stopped abruptly.

"You louse, louse—John is a louse, a big fat louse on a little gray mouse."

She looked up at the big man and grinned—an inane, foolish kind of grin. Her mood changed suddenly. The expression on her face became one of utmost seriousness. She suddenly charged away from the man and ran to the other side of the large reception room. She faced the wall and talked to herself in a barely audible whisper.

"He won't give me anything. He's big and fat and mean and why won't he give Lisa the crayons? He would give them to Muriel. He likes the Muriel me—but today I'm Lisa me, Lisa me."

Then she broke into a hop-skip-and-a-jump, quickly running around the walls of the room.

"Lisa, Lisa, is my name—today I'm the same—the same—the same, the same."

"May I speak to you, John?"

John turned to the tall, thin, teenage boy. David wore horn-rimmed glasses, was fastidiously dressed in a gray tweed suit, and conveyed the impression of utmost seriousness and dedication to intellectual pursuit. His pinched, thin, white face seemed too small for his long body. He spoke with the utmost precision.

"Why, yes, David. What would you like to say?"

"Thank you for your indulgence. Of late it has become increasingly difficult to find ears for my words. I've been studying your patient, or, since you are not a physician, shall I say student. I have come to several conclusions, which I feel time and further study by your staff will validate. Lisa is schizophrenic and is a child—I would say approximately twelve years of age. Therefore, my diagnosis would be childhood schizophrenia, undoubtedly of the chronic variety. However, diagnostic work is no challenge to me. I prefer to study the dynamic aspect of a particular case. Do you follow me?"

"Yes. Yes, indeed I do." John shook his head affirmatively.

"Good. Then I will continue."

Lisa was still hopping and skipping around the room, now periodically emitting a loud war whoop.

David chose his words carefully, the effort graphically demonstrated by his eyes and mouth. "Lisa has a most difficult time with authority or authoritarian figures. It is therefore extremely important that you adopt an attitude of complete permissiveness in your relationship with her. You must realize that this child has utmost difficulty with her emotions. Now, it is my belief that this difficulty is related to her obsession with speaking in rhymes. The rhyming serves as a decoy or camouflage for what she actually feels. I therefore think that you should not have refused her the crayons, even though she marked the wall."

Lisa stopped skipping and walked over to them.

"John, John, don't be gone—don't be gone."

"I'll see you later, David." He patted David on the shoulder.

The boy lurched away and screamed, "You touched me, you boor, you unmitigated fool—you touched me! Do you want to kill me? A touch can kill—you bastard, you rotten bastard!" His face was contorted with rage. He turned and left them, muttering to himself, "The touch that kills, the touch that kills," and carefully examining his shoulder.

—◁◁◖◗▷▷—

Can we sit down and talk a while?"

"Dr. White, I submitted to extensive testing, interviewing, and other such nonsense when I first came here, a year ago. I also spoke to you on occasion after that. Somehow I thought I'd go along with the routine here. New place—all right, I'd go along with the indignities. But there's a limit, even to cooperation—and, frankly, I don't care for more interviewing."

"You felt, New place, get off to a new start."

"Well, I suppose you could say that."

"David, it's not more interviewing I'm interested in. It's talking things over so that perhaps I can help you. After all, that's what we're both here for."

"You call me David—but I call you Dr. White."

"You don't have to."

"What do you mean?"

"You can call me Alan."

"All right, Alan." He smiled. "Let me think about it. When I'm ready, we'll talk."

"Suits me—You know where to find me; I'll be available."

"Suits me too." He walked out of the day room to the library.

She walked to where he was standing and placed herself directly in front of him. She looked up into his eyes and didn't budge. He stared back at her. In a completely serious voice she said, "Hello, hello, kiddo, kiddo."

He smiled. "Kiddo, hello, hello, kiddo."

She felt encouraged—and smiled ever so slightly at him.

"Me, the name; Lisa, the same."

For a minute he was puzzled, but when she repeated, "Me, the name; Lisa, the same," he realized she was asking him a question and then he caught on and answered.

"Me, the same; David, the name."

This time she smiled fully, and it wasn't a silly smile.

────

She passed David working at his table. On it was a large drawing of a clock.

Then she skipped about the room, chanting in a loud voice.

"Dockety dock, clock, clock; dockety dockety, clock clock clock.

"Hockety clock, dockety hock. Hock, hock; dock, dock."

Then she skipped over to John, who was sitting at the other end of the room. First she just stood in front of him. After a few minutes she slowly rocked from foot to foot. Five minutes later she rocked and chanted, this time in a low voice that only John could hear.

"Rockety rock, clock clock—

dickety—rickety—lock lock."

John started to say something, but she ran off on a tour around the room.

He spent days poring over books. There were physics books, math texts, engineering manuals, and books on horology. When he wasn't reading, he spent hours at a drawing board, making elaborate plans of watch and clock mechanisms.

Alan made several attempts to discuss his work with him, but David remained seclusive. At times he ignored Alan. At other times he said, "You're not really interested," or, "You wouldn't understand."

Then one day he picked up the plans he had drawn and locked them in his foot locker. From that time, he began to make more frequent visits to the day room.

Do you have a watch?"

"Yes." He held out his wrist.

"Don't touch me." There was panic in his voice. "Please, don't touch me."

The man let his hand drop back to his side.

"Oh, you can hold your hand up. I'd love to see your watch— but let's not touch." He laughed a small, apprehensive laugh.

The man held his hand up again. David looked at the watch but made sure not to touch the man.

"That's not a very interesting timepiece. Is it the only one you own?"

"I have another, but right now it's not working."

"Oh? What kind is *it?*"

"A small, automatic, waterproof watch. I don't recall the make."

"I see. Probably not very good either. Do you know what kind of eccentric it uses?"

"Eccentric?"

"Yes—the rotor, the winding gear."

"I really don't know."

"Probably on a one-hundred-and-eighty-degree track. The better watches rotate fully, three hundred and sixty degrees."

"I see."

"Do you?" He stared at the man's eyes. "I don't think you do. So few people do. But I'll tell you anyway. There are automatic systems that work by bearings rather than rotor."

"How interesting."

David looked at him skeptically and said, "Perhaps we'll see each other again later; I have to spend a little time observing Lisa now."

"Could I possibly detain you for just a few minutes?"

"Detain me?" He rather liked the expression. "Yes, I suppose I could allow myself to be detained for several minutes."

"Tell me, are you interested in clocks, too?"

"Of course, I'm interested in watches, clocks, sundials—timepieces of all kinds. As a matter of fact, I had my clock execution dream last night."

"Clock execution dream?"

"I thought you would be interested. Frankly, I think you people put too much stress on dreams."

"Oh? Would you tell it to me anyway?"

"Yes, why not? This is a repetitive dream; I've had it time and again. It is always identical; only the characters are different."

"I see."

"No, you don't, but after I tell you, you will see.

"There's a big clock on a spike set in a large white bathtub. The tub is ten times larger than an ordinary one. The hands are huge, exquisitely sharp blades. I sit on a plush perch on the large hand. The face is white enamel. The numerals are sparkling diamonds. The movement is made by Patek Philippe. There are holes throughout the face to accommodate the heads of people sitting on little elevated stools on the other side of the clock. At ten o'clock the execution begins. The large hand, minute by minute, cuts through each neck, cutting off heads. The blood and heads fall into the bathtub."

"Who are the people?"

"They vary. Last night it was John." He pointed to the big man. "It was John—over and over again John—eight times. Who knows? Tonight maybe it will be you."

He walked away whistling.

———

Did you analyze my dream—or does it require further study?"

"Neither."

"Neither?" He was interested now. "Meaning what?"

"A dream has meaning only in terms of the dreamer's symbols."

"Sounds like double talk. Did you at least discern that I was crazy?"

"Crazy?"

"Yes, crazy, or—if you prefer—psychotic—though there's something vulgar about the word 'psychotic.' I prefer 'crazy'—more direct and at the same time homey.

"But what about my dream? You must have thought about it. Or will you evade my question with either more double talk or psychiatric gibberish?"

"You sound angry in your dream—cutting off heads that way. Specifically, you sound angry at John—at least in the last dream you told me. And you sound angry now, too."

He laughed a high-pitched, forced laugh full of mockery. "Brilliant, a brilliant analysis. Killing—hostility—John, anger at John. But how about the fiendish execution machine—the clock death dealer—the bathtub of heads and blood? Surely, surely, you detect the bizarre formulations of paranoid ideation, the intricate workings of a schizophrenic mind."

"Labels never interested me particularly."

"Well, what *does* interest you?"

"People, and what makes them tick."

"People ticking. I like that. Perhaps you *can* understand. I'll tell you an aspect of my clock dream that you did not think of." He waited patiently.

"The second-by-second, minute-by-minute cutting off of heads happens to all of us all of the time. The clock blades represent time, and the victims are all of us; and time slowly, slowly cuts us down—and there is no stopping it—no slowing it. On and on it goes, most accurately and effectively concentrating on batch after batch of victims from the second they are born. There is no escape."

They were silent.

—◆—

You said nothing when I interpreted my dream to you yesterday."

"That's right, I said nothing."

"Are you trying to get me angry?"

"No. I will not attempt to manipulate you in any way."

"Thanks," he said acidly.

After a few moments of silence he looked up. "Well, how come you said nothing?"

"Well, what do you think about it?"

"If you have to stay on good terms with me, don't touch me; don't touch me, and don't get Talmudic with me."

"I haven't touched you."

"That's true—but no Talmud, please."

"Talmud?"

"Stop being cute. You know what I mean. The business of

answering a question with another question, this psychiatric, 'Well, what do you think about it?' So how come you *did* say nothing?"

"I wanted to give it some thought."

"Did you?"

"Yes, I did."

Now he spoke in a soft, childlike voice. There even seemed to be a slight tremor in his voice. "Alan, will you tell me *anything?*"

"All right, I will." He chose his words carefully, speaking very slowly. "I think you're afraid of death—terribly afraid."

"Of course, I am. Who isn't?"

"Now *you're* getting Talmudic."

David laughed a full, hearty laugh. Then he spoke. "I know that you know I'm afraid of death. You knew from the start how I can't stand to be touched—but the dream—I'm talking about the dream."

"So am I."

"Oh?" His eyebrow went up.

"Yes, it shows up in two ways. First, you're sitting on the blade killing your enemies—which will make you feel safer. And, secondly, *you're* sitting *on* the blade—controlling death and life."

"Enough, enough! I've had enough now. I'll see you later." He walked away.

———

Sitting here talking to you reminds me of the first time they brought me to a psychiatrist."

"Oh?"

"Yes. You know—my first consultation." He laughed bitterly. "I was ten years old."

"What about it? How did it go?"

"When we got to the house, a big brownstone—just as we got there—a young girl, about eighteen, ran down the stairs—

and into the street. A second later a very old, bent woman came running after her yelling, 'Come back.' But the young girl was way out of her reach. The old lady yelled, and I remember the exact words—'If you don't come back for your shock treatments, they will put you away.' She yelled back, 'Grandma, I'm afraid. I can't. When I'm ready—not now—not now, please.' "

"How'd you feel?"

He ignored the question and went on with the story. "She didn't come back. A little crowd gathered, and they all watched. In no time at all the girl was a block away. The old woman kept chasing her but couldn't possibly catch up. Everybody looked—but nobody helped; they just stood and watched. You know what I think?"

"What?"

"I think everybody wanted to see that girl get away. They were hoping she'd escape."

"Did you?"

"Yes."

"Then what happened?"

"I went in but hardly spoke to the psychiatrist at all. You know what he said?"

"What?"

"That I'd be all right—nothing serious—for them not to worry. An idiot—an M.D. idiot!"

"Are you angry with me, David?"

"What do you mean?"

"Would you like to call me an idiot? Would you like to run from here? You know—like the girl?"

"That's a crazy idea."

"Is it?"

"Well, this place isn't the most fascinating, you know. Anyway, I have to go to the library now."

He got up and left the room.

Muriel, Muriel is a cigar—just like a car—a car, a car."

She skipped around the room quickly and now changed the rhythm slightly.

"Muriel, Muriel, is a cigar—and it smokes like a car, smokes like a car."

Then she changed to a hop-skip-and-a-jump and changed her rhyme again.

"Hop, skip, jump—Hop, skip, jump. I'm not alump, I'm not alump."

John stepped in front of her. She stopped short.

"No, you're not a lump. You're a girl, Lisa."

She walked around him and resumed skipping.

"I'm not a lump, and I like to jump. Lisa, Lisa is my name— but Muriel, Muriel is the same; the same, the same."

It's not the time or keeping time that interests me. It is the timepiece itself. The accuracy with which a particular instrument keeps time is directly proportional to the effort and skill of the creator."

"Creator?"

"Yes, creator!"

"Peculiar word to use in connection with a machine."

"I know. You would say 'artisan'—or, worse yet, 'technician'—or 'mechanic' or 'manufacturer.' "

"Yes, I would."

"Yes, indeed. That is because to you a watch is only a machine used to serve a purpose—to tell time."

"And to you? What is it to you?"

He grinned slyly. "Thank you for asking me. I needed your question as an introduction. The timepiece to me, if it is a master timepiece, is a creation—a creation symbolizing the utmost skill and artistry. Think of the effort and skill involved in creating a clock that is nearly absolutely accurate. Think of the combination of these utterly precise instruments—and I call the clock parts 'instruments'—arranged in an almost perfect pattern for the purpose of harnessing time."

"Harnessing?"

He laughed an almost natural laugh. " 'Harness' is only a figure of speech—a slip." He became serious again. "I should say to measure time. You know—as one measures length, width, and breadth with a micrometer. To measure this, the most important dimension of all, the most dynamic—this ever-moving, ever-changing, and not changing at all—this most terrifying dimension of all—Time. He stopped and then a minute later, almost as an afterthought to himself, said, "If only we *could,* harness time."

"We can."

"We can?" He looked up at Alan, his face a picture of alert curiosity.

"Perhaps we cannot change the time allotted to us—perhaps we cannot add even one extra second to it. But if we use time in our behalf, if in the time of our lives we have freedom of choice—so that we have grown even one iota, in one split second in all the time of times—then we *have* harnessed this dimension."

"That is a difficult thought to digest. I must give it some thought."

"And time?" Alan smiled.

"And time," David repeated. He turned and walked away.

She stopped in front of David, stared at him, then said, "David, David looks at me—but what does he see, what does he see?"

He looked up from the desk. "It's Lisa, Lisa whom I see—staring at me, staring at me."

She smiled at him and came a little closer. He stood up quickly and walked a little distance away. "Don't touch, don't touch—me don't touch. All else will do—but please no such."

She stood still and remained smiling.

"Touch, such—such touch—foolish talking, foolish squawking."

He repeated, "Yes, but—no such, no touch."

She agreed. "No such, no touch."

——————

You made a friend?"

"Friend? What are you talking about?"

"Lisa. I noticed you talking to her."

"Oh, that. Well, don't get any ideas. My social adjustment or any other psychiatric descriptive nonsense you want to apply just doesn't apply here."

Alan smiled.

"What's so funny?"

"Funny? Oh, nothing funny. I was just thinking that I take great pains not to use so-called psychological technical language, and yet here you accuse me of doing just that anyway."

"All right, that's true," he said grudgingly. "You talk straight enough; it was the others. Does that make you feel better?"

"Yes, it does," Alan said seriously. "It does make me feel better."

"Good for you," David smiled. "Can I get back to this Lisa-child business now?"

"Yes, please do."

"Thank you," he said, clenching his jaw. "Thank you, very much."

Alan remained quiet.

"As I was saying, Lisa is not a friend. I have no friends. If I did have a friend—which is rather inconceivable—it is unlikely that I would choose a twelve- or a thirteen- or fourteen-year-old infant—obviously my intellectual inferior. I talk to Lisa only because she interests me clinically. I would hardly bother to do something as arduous and boring as to talk in rhymes for the mere purpose of a ridiculous friendship."

"I see."

"Good."

He walked to the other side of the large day room to wait for Lisa to come down from her own room.

Lisa walked into the day room. Her head was bent, and she walked slowly.

David approached her. He said nothing. John and Alan spoke quietly on the other side of the room.

"Lisa, Lisa, do you want to talk; or would you rather take a walk?"

"Talk, walk. Don't you see—today I'm sick; I'm not me." She walked away and he followed. Her mood seemed to change abruptly. She skipped around the room but said, "Today I'm low, low, low; so, David, go, go, go." He walked away.

Alan walked to him. "You look angry."

"Angry, bangry," he grinned. "No, I'm not angry. It's just that she's hard to reach."

"Maybe she just doesn't feel well just now."

"I have a feeling that she's trying to tell me that she's menstruating."

"Oh, maybe she is. How do you feel about it?"

"Feel Is that all you think of—feel, feel? I don't feel. I don't feel a thing. Now what do you feel about that?"

"I feel you're angry. As Lisa would say, 'angry, bangry.' "

"I don't think it's funny, and I don't think you understand Lisa or me. I'm not angry—and I'll tell you what I feel—hungry. Yes, hungry. That's what I feel—hungry." He turned to leave the room.

"Well, feeling hungry is a feeling." But David paid no attention and walked out.

⚊⚊⚋⚊⚊

She printed on a white piece of paper with black crayon and then held it up to him. YOU RIME. TALK PLAIN—STRAYT.

"Oh, that makes it easier. It's not s-t-r-a-y-t; it's s-t-r-a-i-g-h-t—and r-h-y-m-e not r-i-m-e."

She printed STRAIGHT and RHYME.

"Can you spell it out loud?"

NO, she printed in huge letters.

"All right, all right—nobody is going to force you, Lisa."

NOT LISA—WHO LISA————MURIEL—MURIEL—I—ME MURIEL.

"Lisa, Muriel. Frankly, I prefer the name Lisa."

She pointed at him with her left index finger—and then came a little closer. He backed away, but she followed.

"Lisa, don't touch me. Now be careful, don't touch me!"

She returned to the table and printed MURIEL, in huge letters, filling up a whole piece of typing paper. She held it up to him.

"Yes—I see. All right, Muriel. Muriel, don't touch me!"

She smiled a little half-smile and returned to the table and sat down.

Lisa and John sat at the table, the paper and pencils before them, saying nothing.

Finally, after some twenty minutes he asked if she would care to write something, or perhaps draw.

She shook her head no. She then walked to the screened window and looked out and watched the clouds. To her it seemed as though they were running after one another in slow motion. After a few minutes she returned to the table, picked up the pencil, and drew three clouds; then she drew them closer together—then overlapping, and finally one cloud within another. She then drew a big black X through them all.

David and Alan came into the room, busily talking in low voices.

Once again she picked up the pencil and printed, DAYVED. John said, "Very good—very good, indeed."

She printed, DAYVED, again, this time in much larger letters.

John took another sheet of paper and printed, DAVID—

DAVID GREEN. "This is another way of spelling his name—
the way he spells it. Green, you know, is his second name."

She took a fresh sheet of paper and printed, DAVID
GREEN———MURIEL.

She looked up at him and pursed her lips—but it wouldn't
come. She couldn't think of her second name. Tears ran down
her cheeks.

"Brent," he said. "Brent."

She tore the sheet up into little pieces; then took a fresh one
and printed:

MURIEL LISA

and then broke into uncontrollable sobbing.

———

Lisa, Lisa, why must we rhyme? It's so hard to do and takes so
much time."

"Funny David, can't you see? Rhyming stops her, she then
can't be."

He looked up with the surprise of discovery. "That's it, that's
it. That's why you rhyme; you suppress Muriel by rhyming. You
suppress her—now I see."

She darted away.

"Lisa, I'm sorry. I'll rhyme; yes I will rhyme—slime, climb,
rhyme. Lisa, Lisa," he called. But she was away now, far away.

The panic overtook her. She ran around the room quickly.

"Climb, slime, climb, slime—I can't rhyme; oh, I can't
rhyme." She began to cry. "I can't rhyme, I can't rhyme."

And a buzz in her head got louder. Then it grew and became
a voice. The voice filled her head; it terrified her. And then she
became calm. She sat down at the table with John.

"Do you feel better, Lisa?"

She looked up at him and laughed, a deep sarcastic laugh.
There was no sound. But its expression was clear on her face.

"Won't you talk?"

Again she laughed the soundless laugh.

"I see, you won't talk." He handed her the sheet of paper.

She drew a huge cigar and colored it bright red. Underneath it she printed:

I AM MURIEL NOW.

———

I had a peculiar dream last night."

"Oh? Would you care to tell me about it?"

"Yes, I will tell you. I searched and searched. It was terribly hard. But then I found it—the Lost Continent. It was a vast place and yet it was small. There were only thin, tall people there. They all wore glasses and were immaculately clean and young. Everybody knew that they must not touch each other. I felt that I'd found—well, as if I'd found home."

"You were comfortable there."

"Yes, I was comfortable there," he said, softly.

"Everybody in the dream sounds like you—at least from the outward description."

"I suppose you could say that.

"Say, do you think it's because I would like to find a place— that is for me? You know, a place where all the others, the you's, would be strangers."

"That may be," Alan replied gently. "But, as you said, the continent was a lost one. Perhaps, David, it would be easier to get to be able to live in this, the world that isn't lost."

"Perhaps, but I don't know." He shook his head as if to clear it. "I mean I'll have to think about it some more."

———

Lisa's heads poked through the holes. There was only one Lisa sitting on a high stool behind the clock. But she had eight faces, and each of them wore a different expression. One looked silly;

another was frightened; the third had a crafty look, and the fourth laughed a high-pitched screaming kind of laugh. He couldn't make out the expressions on the other four but knew that they were all different. Then the sixth from the numeral twelve—and he thought, Twelve noon or twelve midnight—started to talk. "David, I'll talk to you, because that is what I like to do." The first face came into focus. It smiled warmly, even tenderly. He thought of his teddy bear—and its soft cloth ear.

Then ten o'clock rang out and the hands started to move. But a funny thing happened. All the heads came into focus, and the faces looked sweet and gentle. And the hands stopped. He yelled, "Go on, go on!" But they wouldn't budge. He pleaded. "Please, go on." But they didn't move. Then he screamed, "Oh, God, my God!"

His screaming woke him. He was drenched in sweat. He felt very stiff. This was followed by an unfamiliar funny feeling, and then he became very frightened. He quickly stuck his hand under the pillow and found the soft ear of the ancient teddy bear. He brushed his nose, then his eyelids, and then his lips with it. It made him feel better.

Before too long he forgot the nightmare and fell asleep.

——————

He sat at the table reading the math book.

She slipped the note on the table and then stood still. He read it.

PLAY WIT ME.

He looked up at her.

With controlled anger he said, "How stupid can you be! It's 'with' not 'wit'—with, with, not wit. Now, go, leave me be."

She turned around and started to walk away—but suddenly turned again and approached him. But she had changed, looked different, and he got up, a little frightened, ready to leave the room.

"Leave me, be me. David, shmavid, shmavid David."

"Play, play another day," he said, trying to placate her.

But she continued bitterly, "David shmavid—shmavid David."

"All right!" He clenched his teeth. "Lisa, shmisa, shmisa, Lisa."

He turned and left the room.

Finish squawking and talking. Finish talking and squawking. Skipping, jumping, jumping, skipping—that's what I want to do.

"David, skip and jump with me, and I'll skip and jump with you."

"I won't skip and I won't jump, but I'll walk while we talk."

"No squawk talk, no talk squawk—but let's walk, let's walk."

They walked around the day room and said nothing. They were careful not to touch each other.

A nurse told him that Lisa did not feel well and could not come down to the day room. David sat down in an easy chair in one of the small side rooms. After several minutes Alan walked in and sat a short distance from him.

"A penny for your thoughts."

"These are worth considerably less than that."

"I see."

They sat silently for some ten minutes.

"Do you know what I was thinking about when you came in?"

"No, what?"

"Well, just before I came here—that is, to this place—an odd incident occurred."

"Oh, what's that?"

"I had to go uptown to get a clock catalogue. Against my better judgment and with much trepidation, I took the train—the subway. As soon as I got on it, I knew it was a mistake. It looked filthy, but I had to get uptown—and at least it was almost empty. Well, we came to DeKalb Avenue, and a load of people walked in. I wanted to get out—but couldn't without bumping at least one of them—and then the train started, and it was too late. I stood in a corner of the car; I steeled myself but it was no use—I felt very sick. Then we came out of the tunnel, onto the bridge. Being on the bridge made me feel even more closed in—more—well, caught. I had violent palpitations, felt I couldn't breathe." He hesitated and then looked at Alan's eyes. "I guess I thought I'd have a heart attack."

Alan waited, but David didn't go on. He seemed to be daydreaming—away from the room.

"Then what happened?" Alan asked in a whisper.

"Oh, well, that's the funny part of the story—what happened next. And, you know, it all happened within minutes—from the beginning of the Manhattan bridge to Canal Street."

Alan waited.

"It was one of the few times I thought of my mother and father. Suddenly they just occurred to me, and for a second or two I felt better. Then I pictured them yelling at each other, and I felt awful again. That's when the funny thing happened. I saw this woman—a heavy, smiling, Jewish Mamma kind of woman. She was with her three children. There was a boy of about eighteen, a boy of thirteen, and a little boy about six. The little boy was leaning against the thirteen-year-old, sleeping and sucking his thumb. And they were all talking together. Mostly the conversation was about the little boy—how cute he was—Is he still sleeping? Let him sleep, let him sleep—that kind of talk. You know, she didn't have three children; she had four. I became the fourth. I was part of that family—one of her boys—and the funny thing is, the sickness left. I didn't even get off at Canal—I rode right on to Fifty-seventh. Funny, isn't it?" He laughed. "She never knew she had another boy."

"No. I don't think it's funny at all."

His face became serious again. "I'm going to take a walk in the yard now."

"Would you like me along?"

"As you wish."

They got up and left the room.

⸻

He sat with the large physics textbook in front of him. But he didn't look at the material. Periodically he glanced over the top and stared at John and Lisa. They sat at the low table, printing.

That bastard, he thought, that vicious bastard. He'd like to see me dead—I know—I just feel it. I'll watch. I'll watch—touch me, touch me. Probably says vicious things about me. She doesn't understand anyway—how could she—that silly child—that man—a fool, a complete fool—therapist—therapist and he touched me. How he hates me, how he hates—that coarse, stupid, dirty, ridiculous bastard. He doesn't understand that child. Look at the man—big, fat, stupid, vicious, insensitive. Probably wears an American watch—a Mickey-Mouse American watch. No accuracy in that man—no precision—clumsy, stupid clumsy. I hate to even look at him.

He got up and stalked out of the room with his physics book.

⸻

There was a large clock. It ticked steadily as the hands slowly moved around the face. He stood under the large hand and held it, trying to keep it from moving. But it was too strong and kept going. He hung from it—but it moved with him on it. He threw things at it—it kept moving. He struck it again and again with the ax—but it didn't make a dent. He hit it with the sledge hammer. There was a hollow ring that changed to a laugh. The laughing was like a ticking now, and the laughing-ticking said, "Can't stop me, me me me—can't stop me, me me me." He screamed in his sleep and woke up feeling mixed up. But he quickly got up and in so doing re-established his equilibrium.

He went to the bathroom and showered. He soaped himself scrupulously, accounting for every millimeter of skin surface. He soaped and showered eight times, the entire operation taking an hour and ten minutes. He shaved with utmost care, making absolutely certain that no hair remained on his face. After urinating and defecating, he washed his hands six times, brushed his teeth three times, and then carefully combed his hair, making sure that the part was perfectly straight. His entire bathroom activity took two hours, but he had plenty of time until breakfast. After he finished dressing, it was only seven thirty.

———

She looked at herself in the mirror. The girl who looked back at her seemed indistinct, blurred. She tried to make her more real, but she still looked wispy, faded, as if she would disappear. Then she tried to make her more real by making silly faces. She blew her cheeks up with air. She stuck her tongue out. She smiled foolishly. Nothing worked; the image was still vague. Then she clenched her teeth and curled her lip; an angry face looked back at her—but it looked real, of substance, alive. But the anger in it scared her. She turned away from the mirror—and was out of the room, away from the hateful face.

For several days she didn't dare look at the mirror in her room.

She lay in bed and looked up at the ceiling. A little light came through the shaded window. She could just make out a vague shadow on the ceiling. She put her hand on her face. Then her hand seemed to be separated from the rest of her. It was as if it had a life of its own. She regarded it in a detached way—but at the same time concentrated on it so that it absorbed her completely.

It lightly touched her hair and mussed it up in an almost affectionate way. Then it traced the outlines of her nose and mouth almost as a blind person would. Then it came down to her neck and clenched it tightly. At the same time, she felt a kind of bubbling laughing in her head and got frightened. Then she grasped her right hand with her left and removed it from her neck. It moved downward. It touched her small breasts and nipples, and this felt pleasant. Then it went over her belly to her thighs, to her clitoris. It rubbed her clitoris, and it felt nice. After a while the fear and tension was almost gone, and she fell asleep. When she woke in the morning, her hand was part of the rest of her again.

He lay in bed, and at first he didn't sleep. Then he had a fantasy. After a while the fantasy slipped into a dream as he finally fell asleep. There was a great clock—a huge precision instrument made up of extremely complicated parts. It read four o'clock, and chimes rang out four o'clock. Then a voice—neither male nor female, a metallic voice—said, "It's four—one, two, three, four o'clock." Then the clock stopped. It would go no further. Then for an important reason he added twelve to the four and it added up to sixteen. But the clock still didn't move. After a while the clock turned back to number 1 again, and this time went to sixteen o'clock. But it stopped short at 16 and would go no further. The clock then turned into the most complicated mechanism possible. It was an electronic, atomic clock. It was very strong. But it could not break through 16. He then had a funny sensation. Half of him felt different from the other half. It was as if an invisible line was drawn through the middle of him, dividing him into two hemispheres. He looked back at the clock. It was trying desperately to move past 16. It seemed to move past—a second and a half past—and then he stopped dreaming. When he woke, he had a fleeting thought—he was trying to charge through a concrete wall but made no impression on the smooth hard surface.

He spoke to Alan later that day.

"Do you know anything about electronic clocks?"

"No—but sounds interesting."

"I'm sixteen today."

"Oh! Happy birthday."

"About that talk we had——"

"Which?"

"You know, some time ago. Controlling time."

"Oh, yes. What about it?"

"This business of choice. If you have a choice over the time, you said."

"What about it?"

A look of disgust came over his face. "Stop this pedantic what-about-it-stuff! I'm asking you about it. It's your production, so can you spare a few words to elaborate on it?"

"Choice means just that—choice. When people are not well, much of what they do is done because they have to do it. But if they get better and become themselves, then they are free to do as they please; they have a choice."

"You mean compulsive versus noncompulsive."

"You could say that—though I prefer to use plain language rather than technical terms."

"Thanks for being so condescending. Also thanks for the 'they' routine—when you mean me." He suddenly got angry. "Me! That's right, me. Me—David. Real compulsive nut—aren't I?"

Alan started to answer, but David suddenly got up and walked away.

David, here you are; come with me far, oh far." She looked up at him beseechingly.

"Not today, not today—tomorrow I say, tomorrow I say."
He walked to Alan's office. The door was open.

"Hello, David. Please come in."

"She irritates me—certainly can be a nuisance."

"She?"

"That Lisa child."

"She annoys you?"

"Well, sometimes she—oh, I don't know. It's like—oh!" He
threw his hands up in exasperation.

"Everybody is irritated at times."

"Is that supposed to make me feel better?"

"Better or worse—it's simply a statement of fact."

"Statement of fact—I like that. Well, I'll tell you a fact. I had
a really crazy dream last night; a real . . ." He looked for the
words but couldn't find them.

"A real lulu."

"Yes." He smiled. "Could say that—a real lulu. You want to
hear it?"

"Sure do."

"I had a funny feeling in my stomach and then the feeling
turned to a pain—a gnawing kind of pain. Then in my dream
while I had the pain I had a fantasy at the same time. The fantasy
involved my having a rat in my belly—which was slowly but
methodically eating through my diaphragm trying to get to my
heart. The next thing, my fantasy changed: instead of a rat, there
she was—that ridiculous Lisa child. And her face—that sweet
insipid smile of hers."

He waited. Alan said nothing.

"Aren't you going to say anything?"

"Do you want me to?"

"I don't care. But—if you want to—go ahead."

"I think Lisa is getting to you."

"Getting to me?"

"Yes, getting to your feelings. Perhaps you're beginning to
like her."

"Like her! How ridiculous can you get!" He spoke between
clenched teeth. "She's a clinical study—only clinical. Sometimes
you sure can be ridiculous." He got up and left the room—

muttering, "So ridiculous, so ridiculous; almost as stupid as that bastard John."

⸻◈⸻

He ran faster and faster but knew that it was not fast enough. He had a pain in his side and was out of breath but kept running. The thought flashed through his mind that he should have been more of an athlete. But it was too late now. He kept running, and the pain in his side now extended itself to his chest. It became unbearable, but he had to keep going. He looked down. It was there all right, and he couldn't jump to the side. He could run, but some kind of magnetic pull kept him glued to the treadmill. But it wasn't a treadmill; it was a clock, a linear clock. It was a ribbon of ever-moving time that kept disappearing into a huge abyss of nothing. He ran counterclockwise, but time ran out a little faster—and every second brought him closer to the nothingness. Then he realized that running served no purpose; he could not escape the movement of time. And then he was in the nothingness— falling; falling through space—and there was a clock in his head that ticked off the seconds; time was running out, fast. He would soon become part of the nothingness. The ticking stopped—and he woke.

For several days he spoke to nobody. He went to meals and spent the rest of the time reading his books and drawing plans of elaborate clocks. He did not return Alan's greeting.

Then one day, after nearly a week had passed, he returned to the day room. Alan walked up to him.

"Good to see you back, David."

"Good! You mean good for you. You like winning, don't you?"

"Winning?"

"You know what I mean. Winning—between us. Me being here again."

"I didn't know we were having a battle. As a matter of fact, I consider us both on the same side—your side."

"My side?"

"Yes, your side—to help you. After all, that's what I'm here for."

"Sounds corny."

"What does? That anybody should want to help you?"

"That's enough of this psychology. Let's talk of other things."

"Suits me."

"Alan, have you ever considered the possibility of a radio clock?"

"You mean a radio alarm?"

"No, no. That's just a gadget everybody has. I mean—well, this is a new idea. You wouldn't say anything; I mean, I want secrecy—absolute secrecy."

"Everything you tell me is confidential."

"Well, people would wear this clock receiver which would be timed in to a central electronic device—through which they would constantly be informed of the exact time."

"If they were interested."

"What do you mean?"

"Well, I think the idea shows much ingenuity—but few people are interested in constantly having the exact time."

He did not answer and just sat still.

After a few minutes Alan asked, "Have I offended you, David?"

"No."

"David, what made you so angry? You didn't talk to me for about a week."

"It was my feeling."

"Yes, what feeling?"

"I felt you and John were talking about me—that he said vicious things about me. Did—I mean, did he?"

"No."

"No?"

"No."

"The feeling was very strong."

"Your feeling about John must be very strong."

"I hate him! He's an uncouth, savage, ridiculous idiot. I don't see how he'll ever help that child."

"Lisa?"

"Yes, Lisa. What time is it?"

"Ten minutes to lunch time." Alan smiled. "David, how come you own no watch?"

"There isn't a timepiece made that interests me. They're grossly inaccurate—clumsy junk. I don't like them next to my skin. Some day, when I make one—a real piece—a master-piece—then I'll carry it. It won't be a wrist watch anyway."

"Oh? Why not?"

"They can never be really accurate. Besides, I don't like to constrict my wrist. I'm hungry."

"Good. Just about time for lunch."

"I've been thinking about this business of Lisa getting to me."

"Yes."

"Well, she is a rather interesting child."

"Interesting?"

"Well, there are times she—well—when her face is interest-ing-looking."

"She is nice-looking. Beautiful eyes."

"Nice, beautiful—I didn't say that."

"No, you didn't. I did."

"She does have expressive eyes."

"I think so."

"But she can be silly."

"Silly?"

"Well, this jumping about—rhyming and the rest."

"Perhaps she can't help herself."

"Perhaps? There's no perhaps about it. You know very well she can't help herself. After all, she is a sick child."

"Yes, I agree."

—⟨⟨⟩⟩—

FOURTEEN AND A HALF
FOURTEEN YEARS—AND SIX—MONTHS

"Very good—very good, indeed. That's how old you are now—well, to be exact, a week ago."

YOU—YOU, she printed.

"Me?" he said. "If you want to know how old I am, print the question and end it with a question mark."

HOW OLD ARE YOU?

"I am sixteen and a half years old—sixteen years and six months."

JOHN, HOW OLD IS HE?

"Frankly, I don't know and I don't care. But I would judge about three—no, maybe only two."

ALAN—ALAN?

"I don't know—perhaps forty or forty-five or so."

A week later she spoke to John.

"You're three, three, three; you see, you see.

Maybe two, two.

Poor you, poor you."

———

I notice you ignore all the other people here."

"Your observation is correct."

"Do you ever have any desire to socialize with any of them?"

"Socialize—that's quite a word to use for a place like this."

"How so?"

" 'Socialize' implies freedom of choice with whom you have social contact. You should know about the phrase 'freedom of choice,' since you are always using it."

"Always?"

"Almost. Not always—sometimes. Anyway, since talking with people must only be with people here—how much freedom can there be in such a social selection?"

"You can freely choose from the people here."

"Thanks, but no thanks. There's no freedom in that—and you

know it. It's like—well, like asking about an opinion of Republican policy among an all-Democratic group. Besides which, there's another implication that I sense."

"What's that?"

"Well, it's that even though we here in this institution are all individuals and as such different, being here, having the same problems, ought to make us enough the same—that is, people think we ought to be enough the same—so as to give us the desire to socialize. Let me tell you I am not the same. None of us are. We may be here—but we're still different."

"I'm glad you recognize that everyone is different, because we all are different. As for problems, everybody has them—in and out of here. But sounds to me as though you're protesting too much—reacting too strongly."

"What do you mean?"

"Well, like being here does in fact make you the same as everyone else—and that talking to them will add to the similarity, and as such is dangerous."

"I don't know what you're talking about. Besides, I have some research to do now." He left for the library.

Three days later he returned another patient's greeting and later on beat him in a game of chess.

———

She sat in the corner of the room and said in a loud, clear voice,
    "Holly, golly—golly, holly. Golly, holly—holly, golly."

When John approached her, she stopped talking. As soon as he left, she began and repeated over and over again,
    "Holly, golly—golly, holly. Golly, holly—holly, golly."

A week later the room was stripped of Christmas decorations.

———

The snow lasted more than an hour. They searched all over and couldn't find her.

Then John discovered her hiding place. She was in his coat closet. She stood perfectly still inside the heavy tweed coat, using it as a tent. When she came out, the snow had stopped. She skipped and jumped around the room yelling, "Snow, snow, go, go. Go, go—snow, snow."

John spoke to her. "Were you afraid, Lisa? Were you afraid of the snow?"

But she paid no attention and continued to jump about the room.

"Go, go—snow, snow. Snow, snow—go, go."

Then it began again, and she ran for the closet. This time he put a little stool in the tent, and she sat on it until the snow stopped.

She went to the new poster on the wall and looked at it. It was from a travel agency and pictured a beautiful green farm scene with snow-capped mountains in the background. John came up beside her.

She turned to him and said, "So green, so nice—no snow, no ice."

"Yes, Lisa. Green and nice—no snow, no ice," he repeated back to her.

She went to the table near the window, sat down, and drew on a large white sheet of paper. John sat next to her and watched. When she finished, there was a fairly good replica of the poster in miniature. They took it to the wall and tacked it up next to its parent poster.

She stood back and looked—then said, "No snow, no ice— green and nice."

That night in bed she spoke to herself. "Green grass—tall, warm, green grass." She pictured herself putting her face into it. It was warm and tickled. After a while she fell asleep.

A page to write my age—to write my age, I need a page." She
skipped about the room slowly, repeating again and again, "A
page, a page to write my age—to write my age, I need a page."

John stood in her path, and she stopped short. "Here, Lisa.
Here is a piece of paper and a pencil—a page to write your age."

She sat down at the table and printed,

I HAVE A PAGE TO WRITE MY AGE—I'M FOUR-
TEEN AND A HALF THATS NO LAFF.

She looked up at him and smiled. It wasn't a silly smile.

David walked over to her and said nothing. She went to one of
the tables and sat down. He sat opposite her. She printed on the
pad,

LET US SIT AND TAUK.

"You mean let us sit and talk and write, and talk is spelled
t-a-l-k."

YOU PLAY GAME BOY. She pointed to the other side of
the room.

"Yes, I played a game of chess with the boy—with Robert."

Her face crackled into a silly grin. She got up and skipped
away from him.

"Game, game—boy, poy—chess, chess; mess, mess."

She paid no more attention to him that day.

———

Do people really change, Alan? Or I should say, can people
change?"

"Yes, I believe they can, and I believe they do."

"I don't know. It's easy to say. You're so glib about it."

"It is easy to say, but that doesn't make it less true. People
change; people grow!"

"Words, words—just words."

"No, not just words. People change. Look at Lisa."

"Lisa?"

"Yes, Lisa. She writes more, her speech makes more sense—she certainly has improved her relationships here."

"Relationships?"

"Well, like with you. She's friendlier."

"Big change," he grunted.

"Little changes can be important. Growth is a slow process. It doesn't happen suddenly—it's really hard work."

"Hard work, slow process. Funny, I just remembered something."

"Oh? What?"

"When I was very young—maybe seven or eight—two things happened the same day. Completely unimportant—but I never forgot them. About once every year or so I remember them."

"Yes. What were they?"

"If this is psychotherapy, I don't know how it helps—and yet . . ."

"Yet what?"

"Well, I do like to talk—when I'm in the mood. Alan, do you think—well—me here, I mean . . ."

"Yes, you're changing too, David. And I guess I am also."

"Well, anyway, what I remembered was this. My mother and I were on the train going from Brooklyn to Manhattan. We sat near the door. We were both afraid of not being able to get out on time when we'd get to our station."

"Did she say she was afraid?"

"No, but she was; I just knew it."

"I'm sorry for interrupting your story."

"That's OK." He smiled. "Anyway, on Atlantic Avenue a very old lady got on the train. She was very thin and dressed poorly, but she kept smiling all the time. As thin and poor as she was, she seemed happy. Anyway, I then noticed she had a package. She sat down next to a heavy, well-dressed woman and then opened the package. She took out three dolls. They were small but exquisite dolls; each feature was perfect, and they were very elaborately dressed. She fussed with each one—straightening the dress, fixing the hair—and all the time smiling and happy. The next thing, the woman next to her started a conversation with

her, and in a few minutes I saw her hand the old lady some
money and take one of the dolls—a dark one. Then the old lady
moved to another seat next to another well-dressed woman and
started fussing with the dolls again."

"Did she sell another one?"

"I don't know. We got to our station about then. Well, when
we got out and walked a while—the second thing happened that
I never forgot."

"What's that?"

"We came to this nice quiet street, and there was a woman
cooing and kissing and patting and cuddling a baby in a carriage.
When I got up close, I looked at the baby. It was deformed. I
don't remember now—but it was abnormal; even it's face wasn't
right. But she didn't seem to know about it. She just went on
kissing and loving that baby. I thought about it a lot that night.
Couldn't sleep—that and other nights."

"Where were you going with your mother that day?"

"I don't remember—but it was probably to the doctor."

"The doctor?"

"Yes. Around that time they kept taking me to doctors. I was
too tall, too thin, underdeveloped—all kinds of faults." He
looked into Alan's eyes. "You know something?"

"Yes?"

"They really were stupid. There's Lisa. I'll see you later."

You know, I haven't had a clock dream in about a month."

"In a month, you say?"

"That's right—at least that."

"I noticed you playing chess."

"Yes, I've been playing with Robert Salkin. Not a bad
player—but not much competition. I always win."

"Oh."

"You know something I observed?"

"What's that?"

"I think Lisa gets irritated when I play with Robert." He shrugged his shoulders. "Part of her sickness, I guess."

———

David, David, look at me—who do you see, who do you see?" She looked up at him questioningly.

He observed her in a clinical, detached way, as he would a clock or a watch, but said nothing.

"David, David—say to me; say to me what you see."

After she repeated the rhyme some ten times, he finally answered. "A girl, a girl—I see a girl. Who looks like a pearl—a small black pearl."

"A girl, a girl—a small black pearl. Girl, pearl; pearl, girl.

"Pearl, girl; girl, pearl. I'm a girl, a pearl—a black girl pearl."

She ran to the other side of the room.

"John, John—I'm a girl, a girl—a pearl of a girl."

David sat by himself at the table thinking of rhymes. It was more difficult than he had anticipated, and such silly things came up: Come away with me—just you and me—away, far away, to a distant sea.

Then he changed it: Come away with me to a distant sea, a distant sea.

Then he thought, slime, slime—climb, chime, dime dime—girl, pearl, pearl girl. A distant land—foreign sand—no touching with a filthy hand. Lisa, Lisa, name the same—enough, enough of this stuffy stuff—stuffy stuff.

He smiled to himself. Enough of this stuffy stuff, indeed—enough of this nonsense.

He got up and went to the library. For a while he sat and did nothing. Then for over two hours he drew an elaborate plan of a clock. It was a precision instrument capable of nearly absolute accuracy. But it didn't satisfy him. He turned it over and drew the face. When he finished the numerals, he recognized the execution machine. He quickly tore it up and threw it into the wastebasket.

━━◆━━

She lay in bed and thought about the snow. It seemed so gray and strange and cold. She pictured the sky opening up and tons of it falling down all at once. She pulled the cover over her head, shutting out the little light that came through the shaded window. She remembered the smell of John's coat. Remembering the tweediness of it almost made her sneeze. After a while thoughts of the snow disappeared, and she felt better. After much tossing and turning—so that the bed looked like the scene of a great upheaval—she fell asleep, curled up at the foot of it, the cover over her head.

The dream was one of the few clear ones she ever had. There was a great snow storm and she had to get to the other side of the huge square. She couldn't move. Then she saw John's coat—it was very long and stretched clean across the square. She still couldn't move. Then she saw David on the other side—beckoning to her—and she heard his voice calling, "Lisa, Lisa, Lisa, Lisa——" She stepped on the coat.

When she woke in the morning and looked out the window, she saw the sun, bright and warm.

It was a lovely spring day.

John and Lisa sat together at the large round table in his office. She looked through the magazine, slowly turning the pages and studying the pictures. John read the newspaper. But then she looked up at him and pointed to the white sheet of paper.

She had printed,

HERE DAVID→

She then took the piece of paper and held it so that the arrow pointed to the magazine picture of a tall blond boy.

John smiled and said, "It does look like him. Yes, it does, Lisa."

She snatched the paper back, turned it over and printed,
MURIEL
MURIEL
She then gave it back to John.
"All right, Muriel."
She took the piece of paper back and printed,
MURIEL—LISA—MURIEL. She smiled at him.
He said nothing and smiled back.

——◦◦◦——

A clock is to tell time. You know, twelve o'clock, two——Say,
do you know about numbers? Did they teach you about numbers
in that school?"
    She wrote, 1 2 3 4 5.
    "That's right. Very good—very good, indeed. You apparently
know more than you let on."
    David spent the next half-hour drawing clock faces and
teaching her how to tell time. Even he was surprised at the
rapidity with which she learned. However, when he became
philosophical about time, telling about it as a dimension and discussing its importance, she lost interest and no longer paid attention. After a while she left, to look for John. When she found
him, she drew clocks for him and demonstrated her new-found
knowledge.
    David went off to play chess but couldn't find the boy he had
played with. He went to Alan's office and told him that he
couldn't find his chess partner. Alan suggested that they play a
game together, and they did. After the sixth move it became
apparent that David was in control of the game.
    "Are you letting me win?"
    "Letting you? Indeed not."
    "Are you sure? You know, part of the therapeutic approach—
Getting-to-know-you-better kind of rot—plus, Make the kid
feel good."
    "You are suspicious; but let me tell you, as I did once before,

I have not and will not manipulate you in any way whatsoever."

"I don't know about me being suspicious. But it seems—well, you're not playing too well."

"Now let's get this straight. I play chess with you as I would with anybody. I have too much respect for you to play down in any way. I am playing my best. Did it ever occur to you that you're just a better chess player than I am?"

David smiled. "Me better than you? Well, seems funny."

"Doesn't seem funny to me. I may be older and more expert in psychiatry—after all, I've studied it for years—but you undoubtedly are better versed in other things than I am."

"You're trying to make me feel good."

"Not at all. If you feel good, I'm glad for you. But I am simply stating a fact. The fact is you know more about physics than I do, certainly more about horology. I know more medicine— more psychiatry. All of us, you know, have different assets, abilities, and educations."

"Let's play chess."

"OK."

They made two more moves. David now had him in an impossible position. Another move and Alan would be set up for the checkmate.

David got up. "Well, that's enough. Have some work to do in the library."

"Just a minute." Alan reached up.

"Don't touch me!"

"I won't—but we're close to the end; why not finish?"

"What for? It's—well, it's late."

"David, are you afraid—afraid of beating me? We'll still be friends, you know. It's only a chess game. I've lost before."

He sat down and said nothing. In two more moves he mated him.

"Good game, David. I really enjoyed it."

"But you lost."

"I would get a kick out of winning—but you know something?—the real kick is in playing—especially with a good player who can teach me a thing or two. Now, how about some lunch?"

"I am hungry."
They left for the dining room—together.

MURIEL, MURIEL, MURIEL, she printed.
"What about Muriel?" John asked.

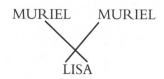

"Yes, yes," John said eagerly.

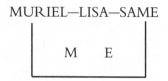

"Yes. All you—that's true."
But she got up and ran off to the other side of the room.
For a minute she stared at Alan and David, who were talking, but then got bored and went to look at some magazines.

Clocks are more interesting than people."
"How so?"
"They're more accurate, more predictable, and just plain more interesting."
"They're more intricate."

"Clocks?"

"No, people."

"Well, I don't know. Some of these timepieces—but——"
He smiled. "Yes, I must admit the human mechanism is more complicated."

"It is—but that's largely because it is not a mechanism. It is not an it; it is a he or she—a person."

"A person. So—what are you getting at?"

"A person. You're right—not predictable because not mechanical. A person—human."

"Human? What's 'human' supposed to encompass?"

"Well—human being—feeling—changing and being unpredictable."

"What's so hot about that?"

"Hot, cold—we are what we are—humans, not clocks."

"A clock is still easier to cope with."

"David, perhaps you are afraid of people?"

"Afraid of people? I suppose so—and perhaps with good reason, too!"

"When you trust yourself more, you'll be less afraid of other people, too."

"Words—just words."

"I don't think so."

He got up and went to his room. He studied the clock plans—but kept thinking of the conversation he had with Alan.

A week later he sat with Alan. For a while he said nothing, but after about ten minutes he spoke.

"I thought about it."

"About what?"

"Me. You know, being afraid of people."

"Yes."

"Well, I think—well, I am afraid—but I'm still interested in clocks and time and things."

"They're not mutually exclusive."

"Meaning what?"

"Meaning, you can still be interested in clocks—just for their own sake."

"But what about death?"

"What about it?"

"Well, I admit it—I'm afraid of it."

"Must be a relief to admit it."

"Yes, I think it is. But isn't everyone afraid of it?"

"Not everyone—but lots of people—to a lesser or greater degree."

"Lesser, greater?"

"Well, my feeling is that people who are afraid to live are afraid to die."

"You mean, if you do a lot of living—then you haven't missed much when you die."

"More or less."

"You know, I just remembered something."

"What's that?"

"I remember going into a movie. I was thirteen years old; it was a bright, sunny day. The movie was dark, pitch black. I found a seat—away—away from everybody. I sat and watched the movie for a while. Suddenly I had a terrible feeling; I broke into a sweat—my heart beat wildly. What I thought of was being dead—the world being there and me gone. The feeling was awful; I felt like I was losing myself—like I was disappearing. Then I ran out of the blackness of the movie into the sunlight. As soon as I got out into the light I felt better."

"You hadn't disappeared."

"No," he said solemnly. "I was still there."

"What were you watching when the fright began?"

"I don't know. You know, I thought about it many times but could never remember. It's funny—my memory is nearly perfect—but that—I couldn't remember."

"I see."

"I'll tell you something I do remember."

"What's that?"

"Well—about a year after that movie incident—I figured something out."

"Yes?"

"I figured out that in a way we never die at all."

"How's that?"

"Well, if people have children and children have children—in a way we go on living just like the branches of a tree."

"It's a very interesting thought."

"Interesting? Well, I don't know. But this I know: at times thinking about it in this way makes me feel lots better."

"Good."

"There's Lisa; I'll see you later."

"OK."

—————

What do you think about what I told you last week?"

"What are you referring to?"

"Oh, you know—my fears. You know, all that pathology."

"Pathology?"

"Yes—my being afraid of death, and of people."

"Well, its being pathological or nonpathological is not terribly important."

"Not important! It's important enough to be keeping me here."

"While that's true, I'm still not terribly interested in your fears pathologically. Setting judgments—sick, sicker; pathological—it's not too important."

"Then what is?"

"Your fears are symptoms—and also symbols. As such they have value—value as routes to what it is that generated them in the first place."

"I see."

"Do you?" Alan smiled.

"Yes, I think I do—but—well, you're so bland. So—well, isn't it unusual to be so accepting of such sickness—of being crazy?"

"Bland, unusual—words, only words. This I can tell you: only by accepting our difficulties can we use them to better understand ourselves—and to grow healthier. Calling ourselves names—crazy and so forth—it just doesn't serve any purpose."

"Healthier, that's a laugh."

"No, it's not a laugh. Let me tell you, everybody—no matter how sick—also has much health, too."

"You mean a combination?"

"Exactly."

"Even me?"

"Most certainly you."

"You know, it just occurred to me."

"What's that?"

"Your name and mine are colors. Alan White, David Green—White and Green."

"That's true; I hadn't thought of it either."

They sat a while and said nothing. After five minutes, David spoke. "The other day there was something I remembered that I wanted to tell you."

"Oh?"

"Yes. I sat here with you and kept thinking about it—but couldn't talk about it."

"Oh, that will happen—and perhaps one day, when you're ready, you'll talk about it."

That night before he went to bed he thought about it again.

He was eleven and went to a freak show. He saw a boy who was supposed to be turning into an elephant but that didn't bother him. Then he saw a man who put needles through his skin, and he didn't like that at all. At another platform he saw a dwarfed, hunchbacked man billed as "The Human Frog," and he felt terribly sorry for him. Then he came to Alan-Adele—half-man, half-woman. He looked, fascinated—one side bearded, the other side smooth-shaved; flat-chested and full-breasted; long hair, short hair. Then he made the error; he thought of himself. He became terrified and ran out of the show shaking and sweating. He still felt odd when he thought about it. But he couldn't talk about the memory to anybody. Not yet.

He decided to try it. He would not rhyme; he would talk to her straight. He sat in the day room in a large rocking chair. A few other patients came in and walked about, but they ignored each other. John came in and said, "Hello," but David did not reply. It was raining outside, a heavy spring rain, but the room was large and bright, well lighted, with many pictures. He looked out the window, at the rain—and the picture of a big beach umbrella popped into his mind. Then he thought of his mother's diaphragm. It was well hidden, and he came across it by accident. He had heard about condoms and thought this was one. It had been in one of their secret places. He didn't touch it—just looked. It seemed all rolled up. But its diameter, its circumference, was huge. He would never grow into the size of that. He remembered running out of the room.

Just then Lisa came in. She immediately walked over to him. John sat at the other side of the room and read the newspaper.

"David, David, how are you? It's raining out—what shall we do?"

"It would have been nice to walk in the garden. But we will do it another time. Come sit down in the chair—over here." He pointed at the other rocker.

She looked at him quizzically. She had rhymed—and he hadn't.

"Chair, there," she whispered, and sat down.

"Lisa, it's hard for me to rhyme. Listen to me—even if it's plain—straight. Lisa, stay." He spoke very slowly and carefully. Now he hesitated—then said, "Lisa, trust me."

She looked up into his eyes. She looked startled and afraid. Then she said in a deeper voice than usual, "David, David, your face is nice; soft, soft—not like snow, not like ice."

He smiled. They sat in the room and rocked up and back in the chairs.

David, hello, you look nice."

"So do you, Lisa."

"Today I'm fifteen David—fifteen. Let's go and look out the window."

"Happy birthday, Lisa. Lisa, you're not talking in rhymes." His heart beat wildly; then he whispered, "And you're not writing. You're you—Lisa, not Muriel."

"Lisa, Muriel, different, the same—just names. Let's look out the window."

He became very pale and he trembled and his breathing became quicker and deeper. "Lisa." He swallowed hard. "Lisa, take my hand."

She looked up into his eyes and slowly took his hand.

He stiffened and felt a surge of fright course from his hand through the rest of his body. He clenched his teeth and tears ran down his cheeks, but he hadn't died.

Hand in hand, they walked to the window.

Notes

LISA BRENT
Initial Intake Note   *September 15, 1958*

This thirteen-year-old white girl initially appears about two or
three years younger than her stated age. Physical examination,
however, reveals a normally developed thirteen-year-old, men-
arche having commenced at age eleven.

Age—13

Height—5' 4"

Weight—98

Blood pressure—100/70

Pulse—76

Respiration—Normal

Temperature—98.7

Blood Study—Negative

Skin reveals no stigmata.

Eye, ear, nose, and throat are
normal.

Heart, lungs, and abdomen
are normal.

Extremities are normal.

Urine Analysis—Negative

Chest X-Ray—Normal

Neuromuscular reflexes are slightly exaggerated but are within
normal limits. Neurologic examination—including response to
light, touch, heat, cold, pain; hearing, seeing; and fundi examination—is negative.

In conclusion, there is no evidence of system pathology. Neurologic, respiratory, circulatory, digestive, and urinary examination reveals no demonstrable lesion.

Psychiatric Examination:
Lisa is a tall, thin, dark-complexioned child. Her eyes are large
and light brown; her nose is short and straight. She has a small
mouth and even white teeth. Her straight brown hair is parted
on the side and is usually disheveled and occasionally neat. Lisa's
expression, appearance, and the impression she makes are more

than ordinarily linked to fluctuations in her mood and personality. She is about four-fifths of the time a pixie-looking, eye-darting, disorganized, hyperactive four-year-old. She darts about the room, hopping, skipping, and jumping—at times in a dystonic fashion, feet and arms disorganized and going in all directions, and at other times skipping and jumping with the precision of a practiced athlete. In this identity she calls herself Lisa, fluctuates from poor to fair contact, and speaks only in rhymes—in a high, sing-song, infantile voice. Occasionally she moves about in a sluggish fashion, appearing depressed. During these usually brief periods her eyes change from a darting near-squint to a wide-eyed expression of dreaminess and pathos. The observer was surprised during observation of the first of the latter moods at the unusual size of her eyes.

About one-fifth of the time Lisa's identity, mood, and activity become radically changed. Her psychomotor activity becomes markedly reduced. She walks about in lady-like fashion, almost gracefully. The pixie quality disappears, as does the affective impression of seeming to be a very young child. There is no longer evidence of giggling and silliness. Lisa then appears to be her stated age. However, she no longer calls herself Lisa. At this time she becomes "Muriel," a name which often comes up in her rhymes as Lisa. During the Muriel identification the patient is mute, but she can write, a skill learned in the A———School prior to her admission here. When given pencil and paper, she may or may not print a few words. Her printing and language are surprisingly good, but we feel that she has even better potential. As Lisa, she is aware of her Muriel characteristics. We suspect that she is aware of Lisa as Muriel—but not as aware. Is it possible that her antics as Lisa embarrass her?

There is undoubtedly considerable autistic preoccupation, but at present it is not possible to expose or to evaluate it.

Attention span is extremely poor, making testing almost impossible. From her rhyming productions, however, we can ascertain good orientation in place and person (Lisa/Muriel). We cannot evaluate her orientation in time. From her rhymes, printing, and previous testing we suspect the existence of a superior I.Q. and considerable talent. There are no demonstrable hallucinatory experiences; however, their existence would not be surprising. Aside from the Muriel delusion and preoccupation, there is no evidence of delusional production.

From observation and the small amount of testing possible, we discern much underlying anxiety. To ward off panic attacks, which occur infrequently, she obviously defends herself with hyperactivity, rhyming, disassociation, and mutism. The hyperactivity probably serves to rid her of the excess energy of her anxiety. The rhyming may be a way of repressing certain affects by a veneer of silliness or nursery-rhyming activity but at the same time managing to communicate. Now these affects may be bound up in the compartment labeled "Muriel." The mutism of Muriel may be a last-ditch attempt to repress threatening displays of unwanted feelings. Of course, the latter explanations are only speculations which will or will not be substantiated only after much time has passed.

From the history and the small amount of testing and contact possible, we feel that Lisa is having much difficulty with the upsurge of sexual feeling and affect in general, particularly anger. Her sickness is essentially an attempt to cope with the latter uncontrollable feelings.

Diagnostic Discussion:
The patient projects a general feeling characteristic of hebephrenia. The giggling, silliness, autistic preoccupation, and affective display of a much younger age level—all contribute to that picture.

However, while her rhymes are sometimes irrational and characteristic of a thought disorder, they are more often rational and indicate a relatively good ability to communicate. There is seldom evidence of a word salad. This, plus the presence of a disassociative process, detracts from that diagnosis.

Suffice to say, then, that the patient is a very sick little girl presenting elements characteristic of hebephrenic schizophrenia complicated by an ability to disassociate, characteristic of multiple personality.

Prognosis:
Very serious in view of present findings and their duration, which is dated from at least age six.

Recommendation:
Continuous relating treatment with a therapist—not necessarily a psychiatrist—and maximum freedom, including mixing with one or two other children in the day room.

LISA BRENT
Six-Month Interval Note   *March 15, 1959*

The patient's relationship to her therapist and to other patients remains completely superficial and paltry. There have been no changes in her productions or general behavior pattern.

No discernible progress can be noted.

LISA BRENT
Six-Month Interval Note   *September 15, 1959*

The patient is beginning to relate simultaneously to another patient—David Green—and to her therapist. Her rhyming productions are directed toward them, as is a considerable portion of her interest. There is no other great change in her productivity or general behavior pattern.

LISA BRENT
One-Year Summary Note   *September 15, 1960*

There have been some significant changes during the last twelve-month period. Testing is still not possible. Her writing ability is definitely improved.

Lisa has continued to relate to David Green (see notes on David Green) and the relationship has become less superficial. This has apparently led to a more solidified transference to her therapist, with whom she spends more time and to whom she is more communicative. Her attention span has increased, and it is now possible to discern good orientations in time. There is less hyperactivity, giggling, and silliness. Her disassociative activity seems to be diminished. The compartmentalization of Lisa/Muriel is becoming more fluid. Though she still uses both names, Muriel comes up more frequently in the Lisa rhymes and Lisa in her Muriel printing. It is not possible to determine the degree or significance of an integrative process at this time. It should be noted, however, that on at least one occasion Lisa and Muriel became one and the patient spoke without rhyming.

Her rhyming activity has undergone a significant transition. Her rhyming two years ago consisted of nonsense syllables meaningful only to herself and was full of neologisms and clang formations. The rhymings at this time were largely primitive productions of primary process and mainly autistic formulations. At times the productions were jumbled enough to be considered a word salad not unlike that of classic hebephrenia. About a year ago her rhyming underwent a more and more pronounced change. It seldom resembled a word salad and began to make much sense. It lost much of the neologic formation and began to deal less with autistic material and more with environmental properties. In short, it changed from a primary-process phenomenon to a secondary-process one. It dealt less with her inner world and more with the outer one she lives in. Her rhymings more and more became comments on things going on about her. The third and final phase of the rhyming transition occurred during this last year and has become more developed during the last six months. This phase has largely consisted of using the rhymes to communicate—to talk to both John and David. An obviously increased desire to talk with David and her therapist has made it more difficult to rhyme. Perhaps a combination of things is taking place. Perhaps her increased trust in herself plus the desire to talk are leading to loosening of the rhyming defense.

Despite obvious progress, the patient continues to be hyperactive, continues to rhyme, continues to be autistic at times, continues to disassociate (though diminished), and in general continues to be extremely immature. She also continues to demonstrate inappropriate affect—though not as inappropriate as on admission. She continues to be fearful, at times hiding in closets for long periods.

Prognosis:
In view of duration and intensity of illness, prognosis, while brighter, remains very serious.

Recommendation:
Continued institutionalization and continued relating therapy.

DAVID GREEN
Initial Intake Note   *September 15, 1958*

This fifteen-year-old white boy appears to be about his stated age. Physical examination reveals a tall, thin, normally developed fifteen-year-old.

Age—15	Blood Study—Negative
Height—5' 10"	Urine Analysis—Normal
Weight—131	Chest X-ray—Normal
Blood Pressure—110/76	Skin reveals no stigmata.
Pulse—70	Eye—myopic, moderate.
Respiration—Normal	Ears, nose, and throat are
Temperature—98.6	normal.
	Extremities are normal.

Neurologic examination—including neuromuscular reflexes; response to light, touch, cold, heat, pain; hearing, seeing; and fundi examination—is negative.

In conclusion, there is no evidence of system pathology. Neurologic, respiratory, circulatory, digestive, and urinary examination reveals no demonstrable lesion.

Psychiatric Examination:
This is a tall, small-boned, narrow-shouldered, white boy, who appears to be approximately his stated age. His hair is straight, dark blond, and perfectly parted on the side. His eyes are large, light blue, and sleepy-looking. His skin is light and clear, his mouth small, teeth even, and nose straight and fine. His features are regular and in good proportion to one another, but his face seems small for his body and has a pinched quality. David is always dressed completely and immaculately in either a gray

tweed or blue serge suit, white shirt, and matching tie. His black shoes shine faultlessly, and his socks are held high by garters. He wears brown horn-rimmed glasses.

He speaks in a low, well-modulated voice, often with obvious if not blatant sarcasm, at other times with only a suggestion of sarcasm and bitterness. His pronunciation is excellent—each word being enunciated with precise clarity. His characteristic precision of speech seems to be effortless and probably a habit of long standing.

The patient is well oriented in all spheres and does not demonstrate overt evidence of hallucinating phenomena. His memory is excellent, and his vocabulary extensive. I.Q. is extremely high. The patient enters interview situations and psychologic testing reluctantly. There is sufficient cooperation, however, to glean considerable information. During interviews the patient demonstrates considerable controlled hostility which makes itself felt by sarcasm and an occasional muffled outburst of anger. Affect is appropriate for the most part. There is, however, some flattening, best demonstrated in areas where considerably less emotion is expressed than would be expected. There is enormous arrogance, and a thin veneer of superiority, undoubtedly evidence of extreme underlying fragility and fear of emotional contact. The patient had become increasingly seclusive and fearful up to the time of his present admission. The latter seclusiveness and fear continue.

The patient is phobic about bodily contact. He cannot tolerate being touched. Physical examination was very difficult, David having insisted on placing the stethoscope, diaphragm, etc., himself. The latter condition has existed for at least five years and has increased in intensity in the last few months prior to entrance at this institution. At present this phobia borders on the delusional, inasmuch as the patient feels that touching may result in death.

David is obsessed with cleanliness, neatness, logic, and precision. A specific obsession involves time and time-keeping mechanisms. He spends many hours drawing clocks and watches and during interviewing expressed much preoccupation with time.

He has good abstraction ability but unexpectedly tends to become concrete intermittently. This concrete approach is mainly expressed in an attempt to mechanize much of his thinking. When he does become involved in discussion, he intellectualizes a great deal and in general impresses the examiner with much overintellectualization. He undoubtedly spends much of his time secluded and preoccupied in autistic activity. While he will discuss general issues, physics, math, clocks, time, and some philosophy, he remains detached and alienated when discussing himself, absolutely refusing to describe early memories, relationships, or his family. Attempts at such discussion result in circumstantiality and evasiveness. Despite some apparent intellectual insight as regards his condition and admission here, insight on any deeper level—that is, on an emotional level—is remarkably lacking. There are well-guarded manifestations of paranoid ideation, but no evidence of a thought disorder other than extreme fear of bodily contact and time-clock preoccupation. Attention span in contact with interviewers is only fair; therefore, a number of short interviews were used to elicit the latter material.

While the patient did permit psychologic testing, cooperation was at best limited. He was sarcastic, resentful, bored, and restless. Nevertheless, there were enough Rorschach and T.A.T. responses to permit some theoretical conclusions. He found I.Q. testing more tolerable and at times seemed involved and even interested.

I.Q. is above 145. General knowledge is extensive and characteristic of a much older individual. However, despite the great fund of general knowledge, a naivete characteristic of a much younger child is always in evidence. The patient demonstrates considerable narcissistic preoccupation and much infantile omnipotence. Identity is poor, as is self-esteem, with much evidence of fragility and a great fund of self-doubt. There is much underlying anxiety and anger, and a very poor ability to accept and to handle these. General fearfulness and preoccupation with death are evident throughout, as is fear of people and relationships of even a superficial nature. There is evidence of sexual upsurgence and an intense effort at control, repression, and denial. There is also much sexual confusion, especially as regards his own sexual identity, which is very poorly established. The patient is extremely defensive, and his defenses for the most part follow an obsessive-compulsive pattern with a definite tendency toward paranoid ideation. While responses and general ideation are not typically characteristic of schizophrenia, they are nevertheless quite florid and at times very bizarre. This is especially true when his anger is tapped. There is also evidence of considerable hopelessness and underlying depression, undoubtedly a function of much self-hate and degradation. There is an unusual degree of cynicism in one so young.

Diagnostic Discussion:
The patient has suffered from a multitude of neurotic symptoms during a majority of his young life. While the predominant symptomatic thread is characteristic of an obsessive compulsive neurosis, there are sufficient other symptoms (phobias, anxiety attacks) to warrant a diagnosis of neurotic reaction, chronic *mixed* type. However, there is also evidence of graver pathology. There is much basic anxiety, poor identification, especially in the sexual area, much self-hate, poor relatedness, and bizarre Rorschach responses, all of which make us think seriously of a diagnosis of pseudo-neurotic schizophrenia. In any case, we are dealing with a very fragile, anxiety-ridden, adolescent boy, who, defense-wise, is treading the line between neurosis and psychosis and who, despite great intelligence, is at present almost nonfunctional. The diagnosis of mixed neurosis with possible schizophrenic underpinnings will be retained for the time being.

Prognosis:
Serious.

Recommendation:
The patient will be allowed as much freedom as possible and will be seen in psychotherapy, as willing, with Dr. Alan White.

DAVID GREEN
Six-Month Interval Note: *March 15, 1959*

The patient remains seclusive, spending almost all of his time alone, with books. His motivation in treatment has been very poor. Instead of regular sessions, Dr. White has made himself available at any time and has spent time in the day room with him. However, David speaks to him only infrequently and for a few minutes at a time.

DAVID GREEN
Six-Month Interval Note: *September 15, 1959*

David has become slightly more communicative, occasionally returning the greeting of other patients and staff members. He seems to be interested in Lisa Brent, at least superficially, observing her and trying to talk to her. He is also spending more time with Dr. White. He is making more use of the library and day room.

DAVID GREEN
One-Year Summary Note: *September 15, 1960*

At the beginning of this period David became interested in Lisa Brent on what he claimed was an intellectual, clinical basis. This apparently changed to an emotional relationship. He has spent increasing time with her, and there has been communication between them. He has even allowed himself to be touched by her on at least one occasion. He has also played chess with another patient, has become less seclusive, and spends time in the day room.

There has been at the same time increased interest in sessions with Dr. White and the establishment of a fairly strong positive transference.

In treatment it is obvious that he is emotionally involved with Lisa and has focused some of his externalizations and paranoid process on Lisa's therapist, probably a function of his jealousy and possessiveness. He has become less arrogant, less sarcastic, and less intellectualized. There is also evidence of less autistic preoccupation, with greater interest in himself in relation to Dr. White and the rest of the world. He has also begun to repress less, bringing up emotionally laden early memories. He does not speak of his family, however, and Dr. White has not pressed for such productions. Dr. White has likewise not touched any of his neurotic defenses (phobias, fears, or externalizations). David has also steered clear of sexual subjects, though his therapist feels that there are undoubtedly sexual feelings for Lisa present. His dreams have become less bizarre and less replete with anger and murder. In general, there is less fear of anger. Anger toward his doctor is now expressed with affect rather than as superior, intellectual statements. The patient seems more hopeful and, interestingly enough, has begun to ask for reassurance as to the possibility of growth and change.

Rorschach demonstrates slightly less bizarreness in the quality of the responses and somewhat less confusion as regards identity sexually. There is still considerable anxiety and anger, and a tendency toward paranoid ideation. There is still considerable infantilism and naivete.

Compulsive cleanliness, fear of body contact, and for the most part detachment from other people continue. The obsession with clocks and time persists, but to a lesser degree. Intellectualization also persists, but to a lesser degree.

Prognosis:
In view of obvious progress, especially as regards emotional involvement with another child and his therapist, prognosis is improved. David seems to be veering away from the borderline of schizophrenia. However, in view of long history and seriousness of illness, prognosis must still remain guarded.

Recommendation:
Continued institutionalization here and treatment with Dr. White. If improvement continues, discharge from the institution and treatment with Dr. White outside may be possible in the next six months to a year. It must be remembered that David is still anxiety-ridden and many months away from the time when he will be able to become involved in the problems of his neurotic defenses, sexuality, and family relations.

Jordi

"Alone, alone, all, all alone;
Alone on a wide, wide sea."

(*The Rime of the Ancient Mariner,*
Samuel T. Coleridge)

For Ellie

Preface

There is no "Jordi." But in my work I have come to know Jordi's of all ages. I thank them for so many things. They inspired this book, indeed helped compose it. They enhanced my growth, both professionally and personally, and above all they have allowed me to share their experiences. Together we've made some wonderful voyages from darkness to light.

I have endeavored to write a book which is scientifically correct. However, the main endeavor of the book is to convey the feeling, panic, suffering, and tragedy involved in mental disturbance and more explicitly in childhood schizophrenia. Disturbances of this nature are, at best, poorly understood illnesses.

There is a trend in psychiatry, the establishment of day hospitals, day centers, and day schools for seriously disturbed people. I feel this is a warm, human, healthy approach to a most difficult problem. I would like to congratulate Dr. Carl Fenechel, director and founder of the "League School for Seriously Disturbed Children." Carl Fenechel is indeed a pioneer, engaged in a noble constructive task. His effort will shed much light on this important new approach to the management of very disturbed children.

A special thanks to Florence Stiller—a warm human being—a great friend. Her encouragement, criticism, and "being there" helped me every inch of the way.

Thanks to Nat Freeman, who made it all possible, and my wife Ellie. Her work has not only largely inspired this book, but she has also helped me immeasurably with its technical aspects.

The End

He ran through the train yelling wildly, and nobody heard him. He was alone in the crowded subway and felt that he had to get to the first car before the next station. He tried squeezing between people's legs, but they didn't budge. Much as he struggled, he went unnoticed.

He sat up in bed. The room was dark, and he had to get to the front of the train. Quickly he put on his shirt and trousers and ran quietly out of the house to the IRT. He had several tokens from previous trips. With some difficulty he pushed through the turnstile and was surprised to see nobody on the platform. Funny, how crowded the station and train could be one minute and empty the next—but this didn't bother him.

He rode from Flatbush Avenue to Van Cortlandt Park— standing in front and watching each station's light and warmth reach out to him through the blackness of the tunnel. He knew the stations by heart. They were really old friends—the only friends he ever had.

On the trip back, he fell asleep, leaning against the glass of number one car again.

At Flatbush Avenue the conductor shook him and asked, "What in the world are you doing on the train four o'clock in the morning?"

He pulled away from the big man and ran out of the train, screaming and crying. In no time at all he was home again and in bed.

He woke up suddenly, looked around the room, and jumped out of bed. People were talking in the kitchen. The woman's voice was high-pitched, tremulous, and sounded very angry. The man's voice said, "Yes—OK, already, OK," and then the door slammed and it was quiet again. He felt like eating but was afraid to go into the kitchen. The garbage pail under the sink, with its greasy, gaping, smelly hole frightened him awfully.

Shaking miserably, he finally opened the door and walked into the room backward. The woman shook her head and said, "Why can't you walk like all of us, Jordi?" He couldn't answer—the pail might hear him. The big hole was like an ear, and it could hear everything—sometimes even his thoughts. If he kept quiet and thought nothing, maybe he could shut it out and make himself safe.

He gulped down his orange juice and ran out of the house. He made it—he was safe again—but he had to be careful of the garbage pails on the street.

And then he remembered that he forgot his jiggler. He had to have his jiggler if he wanted to get by the garbage cans safely. He knew that he had to face the woman again. She just couldn't understand why he wouldn't talk. Sometimes she hugged and kissed him. Sometimes she gave up and shook him.

He marveled at her fearlessness. She talked in front of the can, even picked it up and shook it. But her voice—when that voice got loud and angry, the whole room shook. It felt like he would be crushed by it. It went through him and made him shake and scream inside—stop, stop, stop, stop, stop, but her voice would go on. Sometimes, though, the man's voice, which was kind of deep and smooth, would say, "Stop," and her voice stopped.

He tiptoed into the house, but she saw him and said, "God, Jordi, walk like the rest of us." He took the doorknob attached to a long string and ran past her out of the house. He had his jiggler and was now truly safe.

He let the jiggler hang down in front of him and waited. Soon it would tell his feet where to go. Funny, how his feet followed the jiggler without his even thinking about them. He walked and walked and felt that he was all alone even though there were people here and there.

His feet finally came to the jiggler's destination. There it was—
a water tower, very high—sitting up there in the clouds, alone
and quiet. He looked at the tower, and it made him feel good
inside. He stared at it for a long time, and then the jiggler re-
minded him that he had to go home again.

All the way home he thought of water towers, flagpoles, high
buildings, trees, and many things much taller than he was. Before
he knew it, he and his jiggler were in the kitchen eating lunch.
Her voice asked if he had a nice walk, and he nodded yes. She
kissed the top of his head lovingly, and he said, "It was high—
so high, so beautiful."

"What was high? What, Jordi?"

But he was quiet and didn't feel like talking again.

It rained that morning. He liked the lightning, and the thunder
was rumbly and warm. It was the rain that scared him. Every
time it came, the same thought was there—rain forest—and it
would repeat over and over again—rain forest, rain forest—and
the same picture popped into his head—only lately he was more
and more in the picture.

The trees were raining down. They weren't the tall, nice ones.
They were short, fat, heavy, and stubby. They had giant roots—
that spread out all over. And they came down from the sky to
look for him, and one day one would come—the one that hated
him most. It would crush him into the dirt. The roots would
strangle him. He would be buried deeper and deeper.

Jordi jumped out of bed screaming, "Let me go, let me go!
I'm choking, choking!" He was out of the house now—in the
street, lying on his back—he clawed the air, gasping for breath.

The neighbor from next door said, "The kid is having a fit."
Jordi didn't hear her—the trees were raining down.

The days and nights passed. There were the quiet, safe times—
the withdrawn hours. And there were the terrors, the seconds of
panic. Sometimes they stretched out into hours, and even days.

He walked out of the house dangling his jiggler before him. He
waited for directions. Three boys passed him. They were bored.
One said, "Let's have some fun with that queer-looking kid."

One of the other boys grabbed the jiggler and began to swing
it around in a wide arc.

Jordi was frozen to the spot. A piece was torn out of his middle. He watched the jiggler go round and round. He felt his head
whirl. He didn't even feel the other two boys pushing him. He
didn't hear their taunting words. His agony was too great.

And then he began to scream. He didn't hear his own voice.
He screamed and screamed and paused only to gasp for breath.

The boy dropped the jiggler and ran, and the other two followed. Jordi's mother ran down the stairs, hugged him to her,
and picked up the jiggler. They walked upstairs with his head
pressed against her belly.

He couldn't stop moaning. The gaping wound was still there.
She put him in his bed, washed his face, kissed him and hugged
him. After she placed the jiggler in his hand, he fell asleep, exhausted.

He listened to them talking and knew that it was all about him.
He was curious but not really interested. The sounds, and the
feelings that they conveyed, moved him somewhere deep inside.
The words, however, were just nothing.

The woman's voice was full of tears. "What shall we do,
Dan? Where? What school? None will have him. . . . I love

that kid so, Dan. He's so helpless. . . . Where did we hurt him? How?"

Jordi lost interest and fell asleep. He was part of his dream now and could not hear his father weeping. He was on a train, all alone. He came to many stations full of light and high towers. There were no people, noise, or garbage cans. He slept soundly.

The sunlight woke him. The same mean trick had been played on him again. From his very own world he was plunged again into this hated place; people, garbage cans—big ones, little ones. If he could only remain as when his eyes were closed all day like at night—but they all had a way of getting close to him.

And he couldn't shut them out. There were times when he ran and ran, and there were times when he swung his jiggler furiously—but they were still there. Their voices were all around him. And sometimes the voices were there by themselves. And they yelled at him, chided him, prodded him, and he was afraid— he was so afraid—and there was no place to go, no one he could trust.

Irene and Dan visited the state institution. They knew there was no choice, but they couldn't bring themselves to commit him. The place looked so forbidding, they felt so hopeless. Their little boy, their first born, their Jordi in Brooksville. They tore at themselves and at each other. But the grim fact stuck. No other place would have him.

And then the letter arrived. Mrs. Harris, the last of a multitude of psychiatric social workers they had consulted, informed them that a special school had been organized. She warned them, however, not to be too optimistic. The school would accept only a handful of children—and these only after much testing, interviewing, and screening. The principal prerequisite had to be fulfilled. In order to be admitted a child had to be severely disturbed—in fact, psychotic.

Jordi was observed for hours. There were rooms with one-way mirrors and interviews and tests of all kinds. He played with blocks, ink blots, and little statues of children and adults. The doctors examined him physically as well as mentally. The final diagnostic summary of tests, reports, and interviews read as follows:

"This eight-year-old white, sandy-haired, blue-eyed boy is slightly smaller than his stated age would indicate. ENT are normal. Chest is clear, and heart and circulatory system are normal. Neurological examination is negative. Complete physical examination reveals no system pathology or evidence of organic defect of any kind.

"This child is only moderately oriented in time, place, and person. He apparently suffers from severe anxiety—panic attacks, hallucinatory phenomena—and at times is autistic. Contact is possible but tenuous. There is an obvious thought disorder in evidence. Although there is at times severe intellectual blocking, there is nevertheless evidence of a superior I.Q. and good intellectual potential. The opinion of the diagnostic

staff is that this child is suffering from a severe psychotic reaction, un-
doubtably schizophrenic in nature.

"Final diagnosis: Schizophrenic reaction—type: mixed, undifferentiated, chronic."

Jordi had passed the entrance examination. He was admitted to the
school.

The Middle

They led him out of the house into the bus. It was very different from the trains and their routes that he knew so well. Then they went out of the familiar neighborhood.

He was afraid to sit, and nobody objected to his standing the whole way. He felt very small. It made him feel a little bit bigger to stand. He kept his fist clenched tightly on the seat, and his body became more rigid. As familiar surroundings disappeared, he clenched the seat even tighter, feeling that this would keep him from disappearing too.

He felt that if he held himself tightly and didn't budge, he would not come apart. It took immense concentration to hold himself together. Each bump and jolt threatened to make him scatter into little pieces. A private battle was taking place between him and the lurching of the bus.

The attendant talked to him. He didn't answer. He couldn't hear her. Keeping himself in one part absorbed him totally. All of his senses were concentrated on the terrible effort.

He was aware that they were no longer moving. The scene outside the window was a new one. He did not want to step into this scene. The handle of his seat in the bus was his grip on himself. He couldn't let go—he would surely lose himself.

He heard them reasoning and pleading, but he felt that theirs were foreign voices. He couldn't understand their strange language. If they could only go back—back so that he and his jiggler could become themselves again. And then he knew he was saved. He remembered his jiggler. He reached in his pocket and squeezed it.

Friend, friend—lovely, lovely jiggler, he thought.

He felt the strength and wholeness return to him. The jiggler chased the shakiness right out of him.

He was still afraid, but he squeezed the jiggler and felt connected to the old scene. He walked off the bus. The jiggler felt like it hooked the new scene to the old one. He told himself that this was just a part of the places he knew—not a new place—really a newer part of the old place. That way he wasn't new either. That way he remained himself—Jordi. But when he saw the building, his stomach felt funny. He wasn't so sure now. Holding his jiggler tighter made him feel better. Then he realized he knew the building. This was the place where he fooled with the ink people. Only this time she wasn't there. She stayed at home. He remembered the doctor listening to his chest. He couldn't go in. He trembled. He wanted to run. The streets, criss-crossing wherever he looked, were like a big puzzle he could get caught in. The bus—the bus—the bus. Where was it? Where, where? He charged into it and shrank into the back seat. He clutched the jiggler so tightly his hand became numb. And then he knew he was dying.

He thought, dead, dead—spread—spread. They fit together. And so it was so. He would soon be dead. Spread—dead—dead spread, he thought. He waited for it to happen. He felt his arm become numb, but he was no longer jumpy. The deadness also brought calmness. The panic was gone, and he waited to die.

But then they were in the bus talking to him. He paid no attention. Dying occupied him completely. Then he realized that they were gone. But now a tray of food was on the next seat, and he forgot to die. He was too busy eating, and the bus felt good. After all, it was connected to the old place.

Now and then he saw a stranger come in. But no words were spoken.

After a while the bus was full again, and in motion. This time he sat comfortably the whole trip. The bus felt warmer—kind of cozy and safe.

He looked around and watched the strangers. He held his jiggler all the time but didn't take it out of his pocket.

He noticed the stranger next to him. Then he looked at the one next to that one. After he looked at them all, he felt a little

bit better. But he still wanted to stop being with them. They
were still strangers.

He concentrated on the big man behind the wheel. He remembered the man on the train. Only this man sat; the others
walked up and down.

Then he saw the water tower—his very own water tower.
There it was, out the window. He got up and ran to that side of
the bus. At the same time he yelled, "Hi, tower, high tower—
my tower."

In no time at all the bus was parked in front of his house. He
jumped out eagerly. She was there to hold him and hug him.

He looked around. Nothing had changed.

He was home from his first day at school.

—

He drank his milk slowly, watching her as she did the dishes.

Then she asked, "How was it, Jordi?"

"The man was the same on the train."

"What man?"

"The man who sat."

"Who sat, Jordi?"

"The big stranger."

"But how was school, Jordi?"

"School, pool, fool, tool. So jiggle, jiggle."

He took the jiggler out of his pocket and left the house.

The sun was going down, and he felt cold. He went back to
the house and put on his sweater. Then he dangled the jiggler
and waited.

The jiggler took him all over the neighborhood. He checked
all the places—the tower, the busy street, the subway station. All
of it was like before.

Then it was dark, and he felt the jiggler lead him home.

After supper he was very tired. He went to his room and soon
fell asleep.

He dreamed that he went to his stations, but, instead of a train, he was on a bus. It was warm and nice. And the stations were nice too. And the big sitting man wasn't a stranger. But then they came to a big empty building. He looked inside and could see it was cold. He heard her say, "Jordi—Jordi, school, school," and sat up fully awake.

He waited for the bus full of strangers to arrive. He heard her voice go up and down. It felt good hearing it close to him that way. But he paid no attention to what it said.

He picked up the dried-out leaf and examined it carefully. Then he traced the veins and their branches between his thumb and forefinger. After a while he rolled it into a ball and crushed it, watching the powder blow away before it reached the ground. Then he picked up a green leaf and tried the same thing. But it turned into a green mash, and his fingers got sticky with its juice. When he licked them, he was surprised at the bitter taste and made a funny face. He heard her voice say, "What's the matter, Jordi?"

And he said, "Nothing, just leaf fingers."

Then the bus arrived, and this time he went in and sat down.

He felt funny with the strangers, and his stomach felt uneasy when the bus left the old neighborhood. Then he recognized a few of the faces. When he saw the same man driving, he thought, train man, and the bad feeling left.

He looked out of the window. It felt as though the streets were rushing by him as he sat still. Then he thought of them as flat boats, and the road became an ocean. Their decks carried many interesting objects, all passing by so he could see them. He felt very important and watched the passing boats carefully. There were all kinds and sizes of people. There were carriages. Then he saw a black cat, and he turned it into a panther. The bus carried him away from the scene just as the panther was about to eat up one of the children.

He felt kind of filled up, puffed out, and lifted. Then suddenly the importance just poured out. It was as though a hole had been punched in the middle of him. The stuff just bled out, and he could feel himself shrinking. And then he felt small, and weak and scared again. They had stopped, and there it was. The big red ink building. He felt the coldness of the doctor's stethoscope again, and knew that it was cold inside.

He watched them all leave the bus. Even the train man left. Then he saw them go into the building. He sat and watched and wondered if they would be frozen by the coldness inside. Then he thought of the building—an ice building, all ice inside.

He thought of ice cubes, and his mother cracking them. He pictured the people walking around in there, cold and stiff. Then he thought of them bumping into each other, and pieces cracking off them like ice cubes.

But then he saw the train man leave the building. He watched him walk down the street. He was surprised to see that he walked quickly and softly, without being stiff at all.

Then he saw somebody look out the doorway at him. He quickly turned his head to the other side, but she didn't look stiff either—even soft. He looked back. No—she really didn't look frozen. Then she disappeared inside.

He took his jiggler out, and let it hang between his legs. It pointed to the door. He followed it. He kept following it. Then he looked up and realized he was out of the bus. He was in the new scene. First he wanted to run back to the bus. But then the sun came from behind a cloud, and the street looked bright and warm like other streets he knew.

He walked around the block several times. When he passed the ice house, a stranger waved to him from the window—but he didn't wave back.

The jiggler took him all over the block. Then he walked through the adjoining streets. He looked at the brownstone houses, and they seemed old and tired to him. Then he came to a busy street—full of stores, traffic, and people. For a while he watched a man wash the windows of a five-and-dime store. Then he walked on and came to an IRT subway station. He went down the stairs, looked the platform over, and then came back into the sunlight.

He covered the whole area three times. Then he went back to the ice house. Now the streets were not so new, and he felt better. But the bus was gone. He looked up and down the

street—but no bus. He began to feel very frightened. Then he
thought of the subway station two blocks away and felt the shakiness stop.

Then the lady stranger brought a sandwich and milk out to
him. She sat near him on the stoop, but he paid no attention to
her. He just ate his lunch and thought about the subway station.
And then the rain started. He pictured the rain trees and shuddered. This time he heard her when she said, "Come in, Jordi.
Come in out of the rain."

He was afraid to walk any farther. He leaned against the wall
and thought, it isn't an ice house; it isn't. It isn't an ice house; it
isn't, it isn't an ice house.

But he couldn't go in. Then the girl came into the hall and
said, "Come. Come with Lisa—Lisa–Muriel. Come, come."

He stared at her but didn't budge.

Then she said, "Aw, come on; come on, kid. John, the kid
won't come. He won't come, ho hum—ho hum, the kid won't
come."

The rhyme interested him. He muttered, "Ho hum, ho
hum—won't come, won't come."

She lost interest, though, and disappeared into the room. For-
getting his inhibitions, he walked through the hall to the edge of
the room. He could see the whole room now but stopped short.
He wanted to go in but just couldn't. Then he began to rock up
and back from foot to foot—left to right, right to left. It was
almost as if he had to dissipate the energy of his indecision by
means of this constant to-and-fro rocking.

The room was very big, with lots of windows and lights. There
were all kinds of colored pictures on the walls and a great big
blackboard on one side. Then he saw an open closet and all kinds
of toys and game boxes sticking out. In the center of the room
was a big table with pencils, papers, and crayons on it. Along one
side there were several low tables. There were little and big
strangers here and there. One stranger looked at him the whole
time. And then he remembered her—she was the same one who
looked at him through the window when he walked around the
block.

Then the Lisa–Muriel girl stranger came over to him again.

"Come in, kid, come in.

"John," she yelled to her teacher. "John."

A big man stranger came over. "Yes, Lisa, what is it?"

"This kid, this iddy bid kid, won't come in."

"He will when he's ready to, Lisa. When he's ready, he'll come in with his teacher."

"Who's his teacher, John, who? Not you, John, not you."

"Not me, Lisa. Sally is his teacher—Sally over there," he said, pointing at the woman still standing close to Jordi.

Teacher, teacher, Jordi thought. Teacher stranger—strangers, the public—a public, stranger teacher.

He looked at the woman a second but then got interested in Lisa again. But she no longer knew he was there. She was busy now, alternately hopping and skipping around the room. Periodically she let out a whoop and said, "Muriel, Muriel isn't my name, but to me it's the same, the same, the same."

Then a funny thing happened. He saw a picture of the Eiffel Tower on the adjacent wall. He ran over to it and into the room and yelled, "A tower, a tower!"

The woman stranger—the Sally one—sat down in a chair next to him while he looked at the travel poster hanging on the wall.

———

The smell of the place was strong and clean. It felt exciting and new. But the unfamiliarity made him feel funny in his stomach. It was like breathing something other than air—heady, strange, and somewhat frightening.

She seemed that way to him too. She was new and fresh, but different. She did the same thing day after day. She met him at the bus, walked inside with him, and was there. Wherever he went, she was there. Whatever he did, she was there. For a long time they said nothing to each other and never touched each other. But—no matter what—there she was, close to him. They were inseparable from the time he got off the bus in the morning until he left for home in the late afternoon. After a while he couldn't shut her out.

After a long time, a change took place. This change was subtle and slow. Jordi was not aware of its happening. But their relationship had changed. He no longer felt that she was separate from him. She and he were one. They had merged—the boundaries of their separate skins were no longer a barrier. And yet a thin line separated the her part of him from the rest of him. Her, she—that part was different; it was with different feelings—warm and soft—but very solid.

And then they began to talk.

———

At first their conversation was limited to one or two words.

She would say hello, and he would reply with a timid hello.

And after a while they called each other by name. He kind of liked the name Sally.

And gradually their talking became more complicated. There were more words, and with the words more understanding and feeling passed between them.

———

He couldn't stand the new feeling. It got stronger and stronger and then would leave. When it was gone, he felt nothing—just flat. But the feeling would come again, and he felt torn apart from inside by it. He walked on the street near the school with her. The feeling hit—his heart beat wildly. He grabbed her hand.

"Sally. Sally, garbage cans—cans, cans. Sally, please—over again. Ears, ears—hear me—hear me. Cans—please—please."

She walked to the can in front of the school. She kicked it savagely; her face was contorted with anger. She stomped it—and cursed it—and held his hand all the time.

"Hit it, Jordi. Hit it—kick it. Kick it—come on, Jordi. That god-damned can—let's kill it, Jordi."

Jordi felt his head exploding. He jumped on the can—he screamed wildly—he stamped up and down. The can was almost completely flat—there was no hole left. He stopped yelling—calmed down. There was no new feeling now—and no flat one either.

"Sally. Sally, no can—no can—no ear. It's gone. I made it go—I made it go."

"You were angry, Jordi—angry, angry. Remember, Jordi, you were angry."

Jordi muttered to himself, "Angry, angry. I was angry."

The word was familiar—but now the symbol, the meaning, and the feeling were closer to being one. Jordi played with the word for days—tasted it, chewed it up, tested it. "Angry, angry. Sally—I was angry."

———

She hit him with her fist. Then she pulled his shirt and kicked his ankle. She yelled in a high-pitched voice, "Louse, louse, leave Lisa alone, alone. Lisa wants to go home now. Lisa wants the crayons—louse, louse."

She kicked his ankle again and again.

Jordi couldn't move. He repeated, "Louse, louse," and then his body began to shake while he slumped down to the floor. His ankle hurt, and he felt bruised and miserable. Sally yanked him to his feet.

"Lisa is hitting John, not you, Jordi. John, John. John is John. Jordi is Jordi."

"My foot—my foot," Jordi wept.

"Jordi, *your* foot. The foot of Jordi—you—Jordi. Your foot is fine.

"John—John over there with Lisa—his foot hurts—not your foot. John's foot. Jordi is Jordi. John is John."

"Jordi is Jordi—Jordi is Jordi. I'm Jordi."
Jordi felt his ankle, then his shirt. He looked at John and Lisa. Lisa's teacher—John—talked to her in a low voice. He heard the word "crayon" repeated.
"I'm Jordi—my ankle is fine. Sally, I'm me—Sally, I'm me. John is the louse. Lisa says John is the louse."
"Yes, Jordi, yes. Lisa means John, not you."
"What is a louse, Sally?"

———

The bus wound its way through a narrow residential street and then made a right turn on Ocean Avenue. It rattled along pleasantly—its age in quaint contrast to the modern surroundings in which it found itself. Both sides of the broad avenue were lined with tall concrete and brick buildings. Here and there a one-family house interposed itself among the massive structures.

The small houses and the bus were from an age gone by, a safer, slower time—not as efficient or comfortable perhaps, but not as slick, cold, and imposing either.

Jordi was aware of it all, even though he formulated none of it in words. He was simply aware of his feeling that the bus was warm and homelike—as were the little houses. The tall buildings intrigued him, reaching for the clouds as they did, but the mass of them, connected to one another on both sides of the street, formed a frightening gauntlet for the little bus to run through.

He looked through the back window and shivered happily. His mind's eye viewed a terrible scene indeed. From both sides buildings were crashing down to fill and obliterate Ocean Avenue. Only the bus and the occasional small houses remained intact.

The small bus miraculously escaped the ever-encroaching wave of destruction left in its wake. Huge pieces of buildings—bricks, glass, and cement boulders—smashed against the back of it. They were reduced to small particles and dust clouds. The bus was simply impervious to the explosive crashing destruction going on behind it.

Jordi looked out. Ocean Avenue was a chaotic sea of rubble. People in all states of disfigurement were unsuccessfully attempting to escape. The other cars and trucks were crushed and twisted out of shape. Their occupants screamed to no avail. But Jordi's bus joggled along unmolested and unruffled. The children in it, especially Jordi, remained warm and safe.

Jordi snuggled even deeper into his seat and smiled happily.

———

The classroom was light and bright.

He watched the drops of rain zigzag down the glass panes. They gathered in the corner of the window, and then the crucial drop splattered the pool in all directions. The water running down the glass fascinated him. He looked through the clear streaks left by the rain drops, and then the thought screamed out—rain forest, rain trees! He could see them too—trees raining down—getting closer to the windows. He remembered stomping the garbage can—and then the feeling welled up in him. He smashed the glass with his fists.

Within seconds he broke the three windows in the room. He was striking out, fighting the trees now. He felt so good that he didn't notice the blood gushing from his hands. He screamed in triumph. The trees were receding—and then they were no more.

Sally just caught him as he passed out.

As he came out of the haze, he heard the doctor reassuring Sally. "There were a lot of nasty cuts—but no cut tendons, nerves, or anything important. Quite a lot of blood lost, but he'll be OK. Keep the bandages on, and we'll remove the sutures in about a week."

———

He went to school each morning and returned in the late afternoon. This went on week after week, month after month. He was not aware of the passage of time. Nor was he aware of the change taking place in him. It wasn't a big change, and yet in a way it was. Because he was becoming more comfortable. There were fewer terrors, fewer voices, less hiding in himself. There was so much going on outside of him—so much going on between him and the world, the world and its objects—the world that used to be an emptiness, a nothingness, a hole full of potential disaster. But only he knew of this new world-relating, and even he didn't "know" it. But he felt it—yes, he felt it. And yet it hardly showed. For, after all, as the months went by, there they were, as before—Sally and Jordi, Jordi and Sally—with only a few words between them now and then. But the words were increasing, and they were becoming more and more important as steppingstones between two people.

He called the weekend the "different days." One Sunday when the streets, lacking their normal weekday hustle and bustle, seemed empty, he had a thought, desert, desert—the big Sahara desert he had seen in the book. Then he thought, desert days, desert days.

But then Monday would roll around, and "Sally days" would be there again—and he would feel full and be somebody.

And so the time passed.

Yi, yi! Yi, yi! I'll break them all, all, all. I'll break them all."

He put his heavy mittened fist through one after another of the windows.

"Jordi," she yelled. "Jordi! Stop, stop!"

She caught him and pinned his arms tightly against his body.

"What happened? Why did you break them? Don't you know, Jordi? Why?"

"I'm not Jordi. Leave me alone—I'm not Jordi. I'm me, but me isn't Jordi—not, not today, not today."

"I'm Sally today."

"Yes, you're still Sally—but me, I'm not Jordi, not today, not now."

"What's making you so angry?"

"This place is like an ice house, like an ice house today. I'm keeping my coat on. I won't take it off."

"Keep it on if you like, but that coat is Jordi's coat, and you said you're not Jordi, so why wear his coat?"

He ran over to the rack, tore his coat off, and jumped up and down on it.

"This is my coat, this one," he said, snatching the blue tweed overcoat off the hook.

"That isn't your coat. That belongs to Robert."

"It is Robert's coat, and today it is mine."

"How come it's yours today, Jordi?"

He didn't answer.

"Will it be yours tomorrow?"

"I don't know, I don't know. If I'm Jordi tomorrow, then it won't, but I don't know."

"Oh, I see. Then you must be Robert today."

"Yes, I'm him—I mean I'm me—but me is Robert."

"How come you are Robert?"

"I don't know. I just am Robert, that's all."

"How did you become him?"

He didn't answer.

"All right, Robert," she said. "When did you become him?"

He still ignored her.

"I thought you were Jordi when you left here yesterday."

"I was," he said. "I was—but he took Jordi away from me. He took him away."

"He?"

"Yes, he, Robert."

"Well, how did he, Robert, do that?"

"On my bus, on my school bus, that's how."

"On the bus?"

"He took my seat, he took it from me. He made me sit in his. I had to sit in his. I said, 'Give me my seat, give me my Jordi seat,' but they laughed."

"Who, Jordi?"

He ignored her.

"I mean who laughed?"

He still didn't answer.

"I mean who laughed, Robert?"

"Now I understand you, now I do. It was the train man. The train man, he laughed at me and said, 'Take Robert's seat. All the seats are the same. We can't waste time. Come on, kid, take Robert's seat!' "

"Well, where is Jordi now?" she asked.

"Over there," he said, pointing to Robert. "Over there, that's the Jordi boy, the one that sat in the Jordi seat."

Sally walked over to the coat rack and took down John's big brown coat. It was much too large for her. It came down to her ankles, and the sleeves flapped below her hands.

"I guess I've got the wrong coat on," she said, flapping the sleeves up and down.

"Yes, Sally, that coat isn't yours. That's John's coat—Lisa's teacher, John."

"Then who am I? If I'm wearing John's coat, who am I?"

"Oh, come on, you're silly."

"I'm silly. I guess I am silly with this great big coat on."

"I mean Sally—Sally silly, silly Sally."

"Yes, Jordi, I'm Sally. Maybe silly, but still Sally, and, no matter whose coat I put on, I am still Sally."

She went back to the rack and put one coat on after another. Each time she put another coat on, she asked, "Who am I?" And each time he repeated, "You're Sally, I know you're Sally."

Then she took his hand and said, "Let's go up to William's office." When she got to the director's office, she asked him if he could leave for a few minutes. He said, "Hi, Jordi," as he closed the door behind him. Then Sally sat down in William's chair.

"Whose chair is this?"

"William's chair."

"Where is William?"

"William just went out."

"So who am I?"

"You, you're Sally—silly Sally," he grinned.

She got up. "Sit here, in William's chair." He sat down.

"Where is William?" she asked.

"Oh, he's still outside, Sally. You know that."

"Well, where are you sitting?"

"I'm sitting in the big chair."

"Whose chair?"

"The William chair."

"And who are you?"

He looked into her eyes very solemnly. Then his face crinkled into a big grin, and he said, "I'm Jordi. Yes, Sally, I'm truly Jordi."

———

You know, Sally—the trees are gone."

"What trees, Jordi?"

"The rain trees."

"Oh? Tell me about them."

"The trees that rain down—the trees from the rain forest. You saw them yesterday when I beat them off. The day I got my hands sewed up."

"That wasn't yesterday. That was a year ago, Jordi—a year ago. Remember the calendar we studied, Jordi? Remember the days, the weeks, the months—years?"

"I remember. Yes, I do, Sally."

"Yesterday is just a day ago—the day before today, the day before you got up this morning. You hurt your hands many days ago—a year ago."

"Yes, Sally, I understand. It wasn't yesterday; it was twelve months ago.

"But, Sally, let's talk. I know about days, but the trees—I want to talk about them."

"I'm sorry, Jordi. Go ahead, tell me about the trees."

"Well, the trees—when it rains now, just rain drops come down, not like before Sally."

"Before?"

"You remember rain forest, rain trees—coming down to look for me. They were so scary, so scary," he said, trembling.

"You must have been angry, Jordi. You must have been scared of being angry."

"Angry, me angry. But the trees looked angry."

"Jordi, do you know what a rain forest is? Come, let's look it up in the encyclopedia."

She read the big book out loud. She read all about equatorial rain forests and rain trees and explained the material to him in detail. She ended by saying, "So, you see, Jordi, rain forest doesn't mean trees or forests raining down."

Jordi was fascinated. "Sally, does it say all that in the book?"

"Yes, Jordi, it's all here in this encyclopedia."

"Encyclopedia." He repeated the word several times.

"Would you like to be able to read this book, Jordi?"

"Could I, Sally?"

"Well, you can learn to read, Jordi, if you like."

"Could I, Sally, could I?"

"Yes, Jordi."

Toosies, toosies—hop, skip, and jump." Then she lost interest and walked over to him.

"Hi, kid, wanna play?"

He said, "Play, play, go away."

"Hey, you're funny, sonny."

She took his hand and pulled him along. But he yanked his hand away.

He thought, she will leave me.

He ran to the corner and stood perfectly still. Maybe now she wouldn't notice him, but she ran after him and once again took his hand.

"C'mon, kid, let's play. . . . What's your name? Me, I'm Muriel. Who are you? What does your mommy call you?"

"Jordi."

"Georgie, porgie, puddin' and pie, kiss the girls and made them cry.

"Kiss, piss, fiss. Georgie, porgie."

He screwed up his face. "Georgie, Georgie—who is Georgie?"

"You silly dilly—you—you're Georgie. . . . Dilly, dilly—Willie, Willie? You're funny, honey. Honey, bunny—money—yummy.

"Let's play, Georgie—let's play. Muriel will show you. You're yummy—yum yum, Georgie."

"Jordi," he screamed. "Jordi—I'm Jordi. Tell—Sally, tell—me, I'm Jordi."

"Oh, Jordi. Lordy Jordi—no more porgie Georgie.

"Well, I'm Lisa—Lisa, not Muriel. Like the cigar Daddy smokes—Muriel.

"What's that you're jiggling, Jordi?"

"Jiggling?" He laughed. "I'm jiggling my jiggler. Jiggle, jiggle—wiggle, wiggle—my friend, my friend—my jiggler."

"Make me a jiggler, Jordi—would you, huh?"

"Sally? Where are you, Sally?"

"Here, Jordi, right here. Come, Jordi, Lisa, let's go to lunch."

Promise, Sally, promise we'll take a train ride all over the old stations. I'll show them all to you, Sally—the IRT, the BMT. Will you come with me, Sally—will you?"

"Of course, Jordi. It sounds so nice."

"When, Sally, when?"

"Now, if you like—yes, right now."

"Will we pass the water tower on the way to the station?"

"Yes, we will go down by way of the tower. But first finish lunch, Jordi."

"Why, Sally?"

"Aren't you hungry, Jordi?"

"No."

"But if you eat, you'll grow big and strong."

Jordi dashed from the table, ran upstairs, and grabbed the yard-stick. He broke half a dozen windows before Sally caught up with him.

"Why, Jordi? Why?"

He didn't answer.

Sally held him closer. He yanked himself out of her arms and ran out of the room. Sally followed.

She sat with him the entire afternoon. Not a word passed between them that day, the next, and the next—not for three weeks. They just walked around together. Jordi knew she was there, but his feeling of emptiness just cut him off from her and everything else.

Then he felt like taking a train ride, and he thought of Sally, and he forgot to be silent.

"Sally, can we take the train today?"

"Yes. We can, and we shall."

After lunch they walked about eight blocks to the water tower.

"It's a lovely tower, Sally."

"How is it lovely, Jordi?"

"It's high and it's quiet and it's alone."

"You like it, Jordi?"

"I like it."

"How much, a little or a lot? Sally asked, demonstrating with her hands.

"Much, much—this much and more, Sally—much more. A lot—a big lot."

"I guess you love the tower, Jordi."

He felt the good bursting feeling well up in his chest.

"I love the tower. I do love the water tower."

"Wonderful, Jordi, wonderful. Now you know what love feels like."

"Love. I feel love—I feel love, Sally?"

His face glowed, the feeling spread through him, and he felt warm and nice and comfortable. And then the feeling evaporated and in its place left a scare. He took Sally's hand and said, "Let's take the train now."

On the train he drew his eyes away from the tunnel and his ever-arriving, wonderful stations. He faced her.

"Sally, yesterday I didn't like you, not even a little much."

"You mean you disliked me, Jordi?"

"I did, I did dislike you."

"How did I hurt you yesterday, Jordi?"

"Sally, I want to be little. I want to be a boy." Then the words exploded forth: "You said I'd be big and strong."

"Oh," she said, "three weeks ago, yesterday."

"Yes, Sally. If I'm big, I won't be a boy any more. I don't want to be big, Sally—just a boy, just Jordi."

"You must have been very angry with me."

"Yes, Sally, yes. Let me be little—let me be me, just Jordi."

"Jordi, you will always be you—and some day you will understand this better."

"I like you now, Sally."

"I like you too, Jordi. But if you don't like me—if sometimes you dislike me or dislike me much, hate me—that's all right too."

But he had lost interest and was watching the stations again.

—————

The monkey bars, crisscrossing up and down, forward and backward, intrigued him. There was no question that his jiggler pointed in their direction. But what if he got caught in the middle of all that iron? What if he couldn't get out?

He walked over cautiously and touched the closest bar. It was cold. A sinister chill ran through him. But the jiggler pointed in that direction again. This time he touched a bar warmed by the sun. This felt different, more inviting, but he was still afraid. It looked like a wonderful toy to climb over and swing from. And it looked like an awful monster that could tangle you up, crush you, and kill you.

He couldn't move from the spot. He wanted to run toward and away from it at the same time. Indecision paralyzed him. His face was flushed, and he ground his teeth. Tears streamed down his cheeks, but his legs remained planted.

Her low voice, soft and smooth, said, "Try it. It's fun, Jordi—fun—a toy. I'll show you."

She swung from a high bar, bringing her legs out perpendicular to her body. Then from the top of them she yelled, "Yo-ho, Jordi! It's nice up here."

His legs kicked out of their invisible trap. "Wait for me, Sally. I'm coming to look at the sky too."

On the way back to school he said, "I was afraid it would tangle me."

"Oh?"

"The cold ones. The warm ones were nicer."

Sally told him how the sun warmed some of the bars. She then told him that he could tangle himself but could not get tangled by it—or by anything else that wasn't alive.

Before he went to sleep that night he thought about it a lot and he began to get the feeling of the difference between living and nonliving objects. By the next day some of the magic of the monkey bars was gone—but so was the monster.

They went back the next day. He looked at them but suddenly realized how thin the bars were. Maybe they couldn't hold him. What if he fell through them? They were so shiny. He could feel the whole structure crashing down on him.

"Let's go back, Sally."

"Why?"

"I'm afraid. Please, Sally—please."

"Let's play on the bars for a while first."

"No."

"They can't hurt you, Jordi."

"But if they fall, Sally."

"They are made of iron—very strong stuff, Jordi. They can hold twenty of us."

"But not me, Sally—not me."

"Oh, Jordi, so you're not afraid of the bars being weak?"

"I am afraid."

"You're afraid that you won't hold yourself up, Jordi. But

you're strong. Look at your arms and legs—how sturdy they are."

"I'm strong like the iron, Sally?"

"Well, not like the iron—but good and strong. Strong enough, Jordi, so that you can hold yourself on the bars. That is, if you don't want to fall, Jordi."

"No, no, I don't want to fall."

"Then you won't fall, Jordi. Let's go."

They played on the bars, and it was fun. He felt strong swinging up and back. He smiled at her as they looked at the blue sky.

"Fun, Jordi?"

"Yes—and I'm strong, Sally. Me—Jordi—I'm strong."

He even forgot to take his jiggler out on the way home from school.

———

Several months later he sat at his mother's sewing table.

He looked at the crayons and took out all the short pieces. That left him seven long ones. He couldn't make up his mind. First he started with orange, then red, then black. He finally started to fill the fish in with purple.

But the point was worn down. He tried awfully hard but couldn't stay within the lines. He held his hand stiff and tried not to bend his wrist, but this only made it worse. Tears streamed down his cheeks, and he could hardly see. He held his right hand with his left, but to no avail. Grief and hopelessness flooded him. He heard himself thinking, can't, can't, can't—Jordi can't. Jordi can't. No good, no good, no good.

There was little of the fish left now. The purple made wilder and wilder streaks all over the paper. This time there was no hesitancy in his choice. He took the red crayon. Holding it like a knife, he stabbed the paper again and again. Then he took the black and blotted out the remains of the fish altogether. He took the sharp pencil and stabbed and tore and stabbed and tore over and over again.

The paper was in shreds now. His sobbing tore out of him in spasms. It was interrupted only by short gasps of breath. His body twisted to and fro, and his shoulders heaved up and down. He felt himself drowning in anguish.

Through his tears he suddenly saw the tattered paper. It was monstrous. This torn-up red, purple, black, stabbed, blotted-out fish was horror itself. He screamed and ran. He could feel the thing chasing him. This bleeding, stumpy thing he had wounded. This monster he had manufactured.

The form and color of it kaleidoscoped. He pictured it short, round, fat, tall, black, purple, sharp, dull with jagged holes and hating him. He stopped. He hit his jaw with his closed fist. He hit himself again and again.

His face was very swollen, but the monster had gone. Only a piece of colored paper remained. He crumpled it into a ball and dropped it into the basket.

He heard the key in the door, and then she came in. He heard her say, "Oh, God, oh, God. My God. Why, why? Your face, your face, my baby, my baby. Why, why did you do it, why?"

He let himself be led into the bathroom, and the cold compress felt good. He heard her sobbing but couldn't understand why.

"But, Mama, I feel good. I do, I do feel good."

"Why did you beat yourself? Why, Jordi, why?"

"It was the fish monster. I had to get it away—I just had to. It was—oh, Mama, I don't want to hit myself. I don't want to. I don't know, I don't know—how—how. Oh, Mama, help me," he cried, and then she stopped crying.

He felt himself held by her and felt his bruised cheek being kissed. He snuggled into her arms. Then she led him into the living room and gave him the chocolate bar she had in her bag. He stopped crying, ate it, and felt better.

"I like you. Mom, I like you."

"I love you, Jordi. I love you very much."

"How much, Mom? How much?"

"A great big bunch and then some—more than anything, more than anything in this whole world."

"Gee, I feel nice, Mom. It feels good in here." He pointed to his chest. "It feels warm and good in here."

"I'm glad. I'm so glad, Jordi."

He went outside and walked to the water tower. He sat and stared at it for a while. Then he walked around it and looked at it some more. After a while he started to walk home. He made sure his jiggler was in his pocket but didn't take it out. Just knowing he had it with him made him feel safer.

On the way home he thought about Sally and wondered what words they would rhyme in school. Then he thought of the word "rhyme," and then "slime" and "climb." He pictured himself climbing the water tower. On top of it he would be away and higher than anyone else. But he would have to come down to see Sally and her and him too. Then he thought, her and him, Mama and Papa.

When they ate supper, his jaw ached, and he thought about it.

"Do you feel all right?" his father asked.

"Yes, yes."

"But your jaw, Jordi, does it hurt?"

"My jaw—yes, it hurts. It does hurt."

"I'm sorry it hurts, Jordi."

"Me, I'm sorry too. I'm sorry my jaw hurts."

He rubbed it a little too hard and winced.

After supper he was very tired. He lay on his bed thinking about things for a while. In a very short time he fell asleep.

He dreamed that he was walking on the kitchen floor. He walked up and back, swinging his jiggler to and fro. Suddenly he realized that the floor had a big fish outlined on it, and nearby lay a great big purple crayon. He took the crayon and started to color the fish. But then the crayon turned into a Pogo stick. Jordi rode the Pogo—jumping from spot to spot and depositing purple wherever he landed. Soon the whole fish was purple—and there wasn't a spot outside of the lines.

Then a funny thing happened. The fish rose up from the floor and became a real live purple fish. Then it said, "I like you Jordi. You made me a nice color, and I'll always be your friend."

Then he tied a long string all around the fish and led him through the deserted street like a dog on a leash. And people woke up and began to fill the streets. He wasn't afraid, though,

because he had his fish friend with him, who was bigger even
then a big dog.

He got up the next morning feeling that there was more to
him. He felt as though there was more of him than his usual
self—sort of like a piece had been added. He looked in the dresser
mirror and felt disappointed that there was no addition to himself.
His dimensions were all the same. He was no heavier and no
taller.

But the feeling stuck with him. There was just more of
him, even if he couldn't see it. Maybe there was more inside
him—inside, where he couldn't see but sometimes felt different things.

The feeling made him walk differently. His feet moved more
importantly; his steps were surer. Everything about himself felt
more solid. When he got on the bus that morning, he almost felt
it creak down in response to his added something. He remembered nothing of his dream. It was as if it never happened.

When he got to school, he and Sally rhymed words for a while
and then sat down at the long low table.

"I feel funny, Sally."

"Oh?"

"Sort of like more."

"Like more, Jordi?"

"More—draw, draw. Let's draw, Sally."

She took down a big box of crayons and paper.

For a while he just drew lines—then broader lines, and then
boxes and circles here and there. Then he drew a series of dots
from one corner of the page to the other. Then he drew lines
connecting the dots.

"Sally, could we fill in something?"

"Sure. What would you like to fill in, Jordi?"

He didn't answer.

"Here. Here is a triangle, Jordi."

"A triangle?" he asked.

"Yes." She explained how a triangle consisted of three sides
and three angles—one between each pair of sides. Then she drew
a circle and a rectangle and defined and explained each of them
to him.

Jordi was intrigued with what he heard. Listening to her was great fun.

"Gee, I like this, Sally. I like to play this way."

"Me too," she said.

Then he took a purple crayon and started to fill in the large triangle—the one he now knew was an equilateral triangle. He was very careful, but, unwittingly, he moved just outside the lower left angle.

"Oh, oh," he moaned, "Sally, I feel funny. Oh."

"What's wrong, Jordi? What? Tell me."

He hit himself with his closed fist again and again.

"Hold my hand, Sally. Help me—hold me."

She held his hands between hers as he moaned, "Oh, oh." Then she managed to get him on her lap. She bent over him, held her arms around him, and hugged him tightly.

He felt warm and safe.

After a while he stopped moaning. But she continued to hold him. Soon she started to hum and sing to him—and after a few minutes he hummed along with her. They sat humming and singing for more than an hour. Then they walked around the room and looked at all the new pictures recently placed on the walls.

They had meat loaf, potatoes, and green peas for lunch. Jordi attacked it with relish and even ate some more potatoes before he gulped down his Jell-O.

When they were back upstairs—sitting at the table—Sally started to talk.

"Why were you angry at yourself, Jordi?"

"Angry?"

"Yes—before lunch when you hit yourself and asked me to hold your hands?"

"Oh—I was angry?" he asked with some wonderment. Then he answered himself. "Yes, I was. I went outside the line." Tears started to fill his eyes. "I went outside the line. I couldn't help it—I just couldn't."

"The line, Jordi?"

"Yes, when I filled in with the crayon."

"I see."

"Do you, Sally?"

"Yes. I understand. But, Jordi, you don't have to draw perfectly. It's all right to go outside the line. I'll love you anyway.

"Jordi, you draw just for fun. If it has to be perfect, it's no fun."

"Perfect?" he questioned.

"Yes—you know—just so, all within the line—exactly so. Nothing—nothing is perfect."

"But, Sally, if it's outside the line the triangle won't be a triangle anymore. It will be all over. It will be like wild—like a panther."

"But, Jordi, even if it isn't a triangle anymore, it's OK. And a little bit won't matter anyway. It will still be a triangle. And anyway, Jordi, a drawing isn't a living thing. But, regardless of how you draw, Jordi, you will still be you, and I'll love you inside or outside the line."

"A drawing isn't a living thing," he repeated. "A drawing isn't a living thing.

"Draw an empty fish—draw a fish, Sally."

She outlined a big fish on a large white sheet of paper.

He filled it in with purple. Then he looked at her—and scribbled the crayon outside the outline. He looked at her again. And they both started to laugh together. And they laughed and laughed until their bellies hurt. Then she hugged him and hugged him and kissed his cheek. And it didn't feel bruised at all.

After several months Jordi had learned a considerable amount about addition, subtraction, and the multiplication tables and some facts about division.

One day he asked if they could talk more about the angles—triangles and rectangles. Sally told him all about degrees in angles. Then she went on and explained about circles and area and volume. Jordi was very attentive and absorbed it readily. But then Sally explained that this would be discussed later on in high school and college. She described high school and college and working. Jordi listened but wasn't too interested. Later on they resumed their reading work, and he liked the way she looked when he read a whole page from the reader without stopping.

Just before he went home that day he turned to her and said, "Sally, you really became a teacher in this room."

———

He got off the bus.

"Hello, Sally."

"Hi, Jordi."

"School is nice. I like it. The public, it's the public I don't like."

"The public?"

"Yes, they—the stranger. I was with strangers the whole Saturday and Sunday—the whole weekend."

"But you were home, Jordi."

"Home, home with the public—with strangers."

"Your mother and father were home, Jordi."

"They were public also—they were all strangers. They were all away from me—not close like you and me now here in school, Sally."

"All? Who else was there?"

"The funny baby and Tillie and Joseph."

"Funny baby?"

"Billy—Cousin Billy. He's a little bitty baby."

"But you said he was funny, Jordi."

"Well—he was crying—they couldn't make him stop. They all jumped around the room—and Billy made such funny faces. I laughed. They made mean faces at me. I laughed some more— his face was so funny. They tried to make me stop. Then one of the public—she hit me."

"She? Your mother?"

"Yes—but this weekend she was no mother. She was a stranger."

"You mean because she didn't understand you—she was strange."

"Yes—but you understand me, Sally."

"Not always. Sometimes it takes time. And sometimes it takes the people at home time."

"Like sometimes I can't understand them?"

"That's right, Jordi."

"Let's rhyme words, Sally."

"OK."

They sat down at the table.

"Cat," she began.

"Bat."

"Fat."

"Sat."

It was soon time for lunch.

———

He looked at the ceiling and thought of the sky, the earth, the street, and the subway station. He remembered somebody saying that the world was round. He pictured a round globe hanging in mid-air and then thought of everybody walking to and fro on the big ball. Then he pictured a staircase going down into the ball and coming to a bright station. He saw a train run through the globe and stop at the station. A sandy-haired little boy got on the train holding a string attached to a doorknob between his right thumb and forefinger. The train left the station and rode all around the inside of the globe. The boy walked from one car to the next and finally came to the first one. He hung the door-knob out the front window.

Then the train followed the jiggler—zig, zag, this way and that. Yes, he was using the magic string knob to lead the train all over the inside of the earth. It was actually working. The magic jiggler was controlling the train.

Then he realized that the boy was getting larger. He had the same face and the same sandy hair, but he was big now—very big. Soon he was a giant and almost filled the whole car. He could tell that the boy giant was afraid of nothing. There he was with his jiggler and his train going wherever he liked. Nobody could stop him. The earth was his.

Then Jordi saw the boy wave the jiggler around outside the front window. And the train left the track, and there was no track in front of it or anywhere in sight. But the train went faster than ever—whiz, whiz, whiz. It cut through the earth. It was cutting the globe up like a big piece of cake, only it was doing it from the inside. And then he saw big pieces of the globe caving in all over the train. But the giant boy and his jiggler led the train right through it all to slice up the earth some more—and more and more.

When he looked at the top of the earth, people were running all over the place, but they couldn't get away. They were being buried by the big cave-ins. Buildings were crumbling all over. It was dark, but the sky was bright blood red. And in the light of the redness Jordi could see the earth and many things on it falling down, down and crumbling all up. The giant had a big smile on his face now.

The earth, and everything on it, was gone. Only the train remained, and the giant boy and his jiggler led it from station to lighted station through space.

Jordi rolled over and fell asleep at once.

The bath felt very nice. It was warm, and he was alone. He pushed the piece of wood around the tub and watched it skim over his knees and then back again over his belly. Then he held it down on the bottom of the tub and let it go suddenly, watching it shoot to the surface. He let the wood float and then dropped the bar of soap on it from different heights. Splash, splash, but the wood popped right up again. Then he thought of his penis. First he squeezed it; then he rubbed it up and down. It felt nice, and it was good to be alone. When his penis stood up, he stared at it a while and wondered how this magic took place. There it was again much bigger than before and standing straight up. He thought, first it's like the jiggler, then it's like the water tower.

After a while he got up and soaped himself all over. Then sat down and let the water get real cloudy and soapy.

He lay on his back, and almost his whole body was hidden by the cloudy water. He pushed his foot through. He could see it but not the rest of his leg. He suddenly felt that his foot was detached from his leg and the rest of his body. He became very frightened and lifted his foot quickly, and there it was, still part of the rest of him. He felt much better but didn't dare lift his foot that way again—at least not in the cloudy water.

He played with the wooden boat some more. It glided over his belly. Then he let the dirty water out of the tub and let in new clean clear water.

Then he felt interested in his belly button. He looked at it and screwed his finger around in it. Then he noticed how a little water remained in his belly button each time he brought his belly up out of the water.

He had a funny thought: Button is to close up something. Belly button closes the belly. What if it opened up and a little water got in?

He could already see himself swelling, swelling, swelling and then—pop—exploding.

And yet he knew with his thoughts, that it wouldn't happen. He knew that his belly button wouldn't open, and he even doubted that it had anything to do with his insides anyway. But the feeling about it and the picture of water leaking in persisted. So he felt a little silly but got up and dried himself. He made sure no water remained in his belly button.

He sat with them and stared at his father. He waited for him to talk. He liked to hear his voice. It was soft and deep and made him feel warm. The thunder was the same way, too. His mother's

voice was high and thinner. Sometimes it stuck and cut, but
sometimes it was high and bright like lightning.

"Jordi, would you like to go to the zoo?"

"Yes."

And then they left the house. He held his hand and let himself
be led even though he knew the train route they were taking.

When they got off at the station, they had a long block to
walk to the zoo. He kicked a can he found all along the way.
Then they saw the elephants, monkeys, and lions.

His father knew that the panthers pleased him most, so they
stayed at the cage for a long time.

Jordi watched the animal pace up and down and wondered
what would happen if it got loose. He liked its shininess and the
rippling way it moved. Woosh, woosh—he could see it tear
through the crowd and everybody running in all directions.
Everybody but me, he thought as he took his jiggler out and
dangled it.

His father bought some popcorn and peanuts. They sat on the
bench and fed themselves and the squirrels. The squirrels pleased
him very much, taking the nuts from his fingers the way they
did.

⤙⊷⤚

Boy, is he angry! Jesus Christ, he is *mad!* Boy! Look at him—
just look, Sally."

He had the magazine open to an insurance ad. There was a
picture of a train wreck and a man looking at it with a startled,
worried expression on his face.

"Wow! This man is *angry.* Wow, is he angry—an angry man,
a truly angry man."

Jordi walked up and down the room. He was too excited to
do anything else that day. He felt this man's feeling. And seeing
a man whose feeling was his feeling in a big magazine was very
exciting. He was so excited he hardly ate lunch that day. He
carried the magazine with him wherever he went for a whole

week. Then he asked Sally if they could hang the magazine on the bulletin board. They tried tacking it up but finally settled on just putting up the page with the picture.

He walked up to the wall again and again. Then, almost a month after they put the picture up, he left Sally at the low table and walked over to Lisa and John. He stood close to them and watched Lisa make the Indian bead ring.

"Hi, kid—hi," she said.

"Hello, hello. Come with me, Lisa. I want to show you."

She looked to John.

"Go, Lisa," he said. "Go with Jordi."

"All right, Jordi Pordi. Let's amble, let's scramble, and let's go—but slow—ho, ho."

He led her to the picture on the wall. He pointed to it. "Jesus Christ, is he angry! Boy, he is! He is—he is sure truly angry."

"Jordi, Pordi, let's play jacks. OK? Jacks, facts—let's go, Jo."

"But, Lisa, the man—look, look at him—how he looks. Boy, is he mad! He is *sore!*"

"Sore, tore—what for?" She ran back to John.

He looked at the picture again, shrugged his shoulders, and went back to Sally at the table.

"That Lisa–Muriel kid is funny. Angry—angry—she doesn't know what it is—angry. Funny, honey—that girl is funny. She sure is."

"Well, we're not all the same, Jordi."

"But angry—Sally, I told her about angry—and she walked away."

"About anger, Jordi," she corrected.

"Yes, Sally—about anger."

He went on. "She is funny, that kid. She is funny."

"Well, we all have problems, Jordi."

"Problems. Gee, that's a funny way to say it—problems. What do you mean—problems?"

"Well, like you, Jordi—when you were afraid of the monkey bars."

"Yes, Sally—and like the garbage cans and the rain trees."

"That's right, Jordi."

"But, Sally, that was the old Jordi.

"Do you remember, do you remember the old Jordi, Sally? Do you remember him? He couldn't ride a bike. He was afraid of the cans. Sometimes he was afraid to talk. He had problems. He had lots of problems, Sally—boy, oh boy, he truly had problems.

"But now, Sally, now the new Jordi is here. He can walk and ride and talk and go on the monkey bars. He can get angry and he can say 'gee whizz,' and he can draw outside the line.

"And, Sally, the new Jordi—me—I know about triangles and I can read too."

"You sure can, Jordi—and how you can."

Lisa walked by. She was talking to herself.

"Muriel is my name—and it's the same, the same."

Jordi looked at Sally and then asked, "Is her problem showing, Sally? Is Lisa's problem showing?"

"Yes, I guess it is, Jordi. You could say that. Her problem is showing."

"Sally, it's a long time, a long time. Isn't it, Sally?"

"A long time what is? What, Jordi? What is a long time?"

"You, Sally. You—you and me. Is it years? Is it years and years, Sally?"

"Jordi, it's years—but it seems longer to me too."

"Sally, it's like you were always. Like when I think of it—it's like it was black before."

"Black, Jordi?"

"Last night I thought of before. It seemed so long ago like it wasn't. Then I knew it was—and when I thought of it—I saw it like a darkness. It was all black—I got scared. I jumped out of bed—and put the light on. Then I felt better. Then I thought, Sally, and the blackness became gone. I said 'Sally,' then I turned off the light—and it was dark—but it was light."

———

Several months passed.

After he had come home one afternoon, he went into the

bathroom, locked the door, and then took out his penis and examined it. He thought it looked like a toadstool he once saw in a picture book. He rubbed it a while and before long felt better—after it got soft he looked at it again before he put it back, and it seemed longer to him. Then he looked in the mirror and saw that he had got bigger than he had remembered himself. Then he buttoned his trousers and went outside.

He began to walk to the water tower but saw the skinny boy playing stoop ball several houses down. He walked over to the ball player and watched. He thought, how skinny he is. But he was awed at his ability to throw the ball. He really hit the steps hard, and he caught it each time too. Jordi forgot about the water tower and just stood there with his hands at his sides, watching. After a while "Skinny"—Jordi now thought of him by that name—stopped playing, put the ball in his pocket, and walked off. He went back to his house.

"Mom, I want a ball."

"A ball, Jordi? Sure. What kind?"

"Kind?" he asked.

"Yes. A little one, a big one? A football?"

"Just a little one, Mom. A hand ball—not for feet, but for playing with hands."

"All right, dear, here's a quarter. The man at the candy store will give you a ball for it."

He went to the candy store with the coin clenched tightly in his fist. Then he went inside. It was kind of dark and smelled sour. The fat man with the red face walked toward him and began to ask what he wanted. Jordi turned around and quickly walked out.

Then he walked to the water tower, still holding the quarter tightly clenched in his fist. He stared at the tower a while and then went home.

"Did you buy the ball, Jordi?"

"No."

"Do you still have the quarter?"

"Yes. I'll buy it tomorrow, Mom. I'll buy it with Sally."

That night before he went to bed he stood in front of his dresser mirror wearing only his shorts. Then he examined him-

self. He thought he was taller and heavier than "Skinny." Then
he sucked his stomach in, and even that way he wasn't as skinny
as "Skinny." He thought of swinging on the monkey bars and
being strong. He said to the mirror, "Jordi, you're a sturdy boy,
a sturdy boy. Jordi you're strong, truly strong."

He practiced throwing an imaginary ball against the mirror
and catching it. Then he thought of doing it against the steps.
He pictured "Skinny" watching him. Then he saw himself missing the ball and "Skinny" laughing. He suddenly felt chilled and
shuddered.

He got into bed and pulled the covers up to his chin. He felt
cozy and warm. The orange glow of the ceiling lights added to
his warm feeling. He let it burn all night.

The next day he showed Sally the quarter and told her it was
for a ball.

"I went to the store at home, but I got scared and ran out.
Can we get it at the candy store near here, Sally?"

"Sure we can, Jordi. We'll go down after lunch and buy a ball.
But what kind of game do you want to play with it?"

"Well—you know, Sally—like I saw this skinny boy play on
my home street. He was throwing the ball against the steps and
catching it. Boy, he could do it strong. He is skinny but strong."

"That's called stoop ball," she said.

Sally went on and described the game to him. Then she described baseball, football, and basketball. She got the basketball
from the basement and showed it to him. He held the ball, and
his hands felt nice rubbing around it. She asked if he would like
to shoot for baskets in the schoolyard, but he said, "No, I just
want to buy a little white ball and play Skinny's game, stoop
ball."

" 'Buy,' Jordi? You said 'buy.' "

"Yes, like my mother buys in the store."

"Good. Let's spend the rest of the time before lunch talking
about buying and money."

Then they talked about the different kinds of stores and things
to buy. They talked all about pennies, nickels, dimes, and quar-
ters. Sally demonstrated them all to him, including paper money.
Then they pretended to buy things from each other.

Jordi thought Sally seemed very excited and happy, and he felt good too. She went upstairs and got a lot of coins and bills from William. Then they made the big room into different kinds of stores. They sold each other everything in the room, and they made change and bought up everything and sold it back.

After lunch Jordi wanted to play with the money some more before going out to buy the ball.

This time Sally tried to give him a better idea about the relative value and prices of things. Jordi caught on very quickly and had a lot of fun guessing the price of eggs, butter, a lunch, a chair, a car, and many other things.

Sally then went on to explain how people earned money and how stores made profits by buying low and selling high. Jordi asked her about checks, but when she started to explain about them, he finally lost interest and asked her if they could buy the ball now.

On the way to the store Sally explained more about how either one hundred or one hundred fifty wins in stoop ball. Then she casually asked him, "Who is that boy 'Skinny' you mentioned?"

But his mind was elsewhere.

"Sally, you know the subway tokens are like money."

"Yes, indeed, Jordi. They're worth fifteen cents each."

"Sally, I used to take them off the dresser and sometimes I just walked under the turning thing without one."

"How did you know about the tokens, Jordi?"

"Pop, he used them when we went to the zoo. He let me put it in the thing too."

"In the slot," she added.

"Yes, in the slot. Then he used to put them on the dresser. So, one day I took one and tried it, and went to some stations."

They both walked into the candy store. Jordi held his quarter out and went over to the woman behind the counter.

"Here is a quarter, twenty-five pennies. This is for you—and for me, I want a ball."

He hesitated, then added, "I want to buy a ball—a little plain white one for playing stoop ball."

The woman smiled at him and said, "That's a lot of pennies. For twenty-five cents you can get a Spalding."

He looked at Sally questioningly, and she nodded, yes.

After they left the store, he asked her what "a Spalding" meant. She explained about different makes and different qualities of the same article and about the differences these made in relative money value. He listened attentively and then said, "Gee, Sally, you know a lot of a lot of a lot of things."

Then Sally stopped walking and turned him around to face her. She held his shoulders and looked into his eyes and said, "Jordi, today you talked to a stranger. You just walked into that store and talked to somebody you didn't know. Not only that, you asked for something and nothing bad happened, Jordi. It came out fine."

"I talked to a stranger," he repeated. "I talked to a stranger—you know, Sally—and then she wasn't so strange anymore."

Then they walked back to school to practice stoop ball.

It wasn't at all easy. Sally told him to be careful of cars when he went to retrieve the ball. And he did a lot of retrieving. Each time he hit a point the ball went over his head. But he learned fast, and before long he was a stoop-ball player.

After an hour his arm hurt, but he kept playing. After a while he tallied up points, and then it was even more fun. But when his arm felt real heavy, he said, "Let's rhyme words or something, Sally."

He played lots of stoop ball after that, both at school and at home. He carried the ball constantly, and on some days he was so busy holding and squeezing it that he hardly remembered his jiggler.

—————

I can climb the bars now, Sally."

"What was that, Jordi? I didn't hear you."

"The bars, monkey bars—now I can climb on them and play."

"Yes, you sure can."

"Sally, it's the bars and things, other things, too."

"Yes, there's been much, Jordi—many things."

And there were things, many things. There was incident after incident. There were bars, many bars—bars to cross, bars to climb, bars to knock down—and they did it. And it was hard work. But they struggled, and the bars came down.

Spring had come. It was a warm day.

"How about going over to the playground, Jordi?"

"What will we do there, Sally?"

"Well, there's the monkey bars."

"No, no, Sally, let's do something else."

"Why? Are you afraid of something, Jordi?"

"No, no," he hastened to reassure her.

"It's just—well." He seemed embarrassed.

"Jordi, come on now, what's doing?" she asked.

"Well, Sally—well, the other children playing there—well, Sally—well—they're small, Sally. They're so small."

"You're right, Jordi. I hadn't realized—you are bigger than the other children. I guess I sometimes forget you're a big boy now. You're over twelve now—over twelve years old."

She seemed very pleased with it all. He couldn't understand why but kind of felt happy because she seemed to feel so good.

After lunch Sally said she wanted to read something important and would he like to busy himself for a while. He welcomed being alone and told her he would be on the stoop of the school building.

He sat there a while, and then he took out his jiggler. He noticed how hard it was to get it out of his pocket. Then he took the ball from his other pocket. He weighed and balanced them, one in each hand. Then he thought to himself, my old jiggler. He put it back in his pocket and began to play stoop ball. Then for the first time in his memory the jiggler bothered him. He felt the shaft of the doorknob dig into his thigh each time he threw the ball. He took the jiggler out again and went into the building to find Sally at her desk.

"Will you hold my jiggler for me, Sally? I want to play stoop ball."

She said, "Sure, Jordi. Here, I'll put it in my desk drawer."

He went outside and resumed his solitary game of stoop ball.

·······

Several weeks later it was a beautiful, dry frosty day. They went to the playground, and Jordi walked around for a while, just breathing in the crispy air and feeling good.

He watched the children on the monkey bars and thought that they looked just like the little monkeys in the zoo.

Sally sat on the bench and read while he explored the entire playground. Then he saw the group of boys playing handball. They were about ten years old. There were three of them, and the very dark boy yelled out to him.

"Hey, fella, how about some handball? I need a partner."

Jordi said, "I don't know how."

"Don't worry, I'll show you. My name is Billy. What's your name?"

"I'm Jordi."

"Come on, Jordi." Billy beckoned, and Jordi joined the group.

·······

He had no idea that four years had passed since he first entered the "ice house."

When Sally told him about the impending examination, he vaguely remembered the ink blots, the cold stethoscope, and somebody talking and bothering him.

After they talked about it a while he lost interest, and they went back to what they were doing.

This twelve-year-old, white, sandy-haired boy has been examined, tested, and interviewed by the psychological and psychiatric diagnostic and planning staff.

His size, weight, and appearance are not unusual. There is no evidence of physical impairment of any kind. There is no evidence of organicity. Contact is good, and attention span is fair. He hesitates at the beginning of the interview situation but soon adjusts and relates adequately.

He is well oriented in all spheres and demonstrates good memory function for both recent and past events. There is at present no evidence of secondary phenomena, hallucinations and delusions not being demonstrable. Impulse control is fair. His affective display is somewhat shallower than normal but is appropriate for the most part.

TAT and Rorschach as well as pressure during interviewing indicate and elicit considerable underlying hostility and anxiety. There is also evidence of an inappropriate naivete and a rather infantile. approach to himself and his place in the world. There is a paucity of general information mainly pertaining to history, geography, sports events, etc. There is, however, indication of a superior I.Q.—a surprisingly good vocabulary and intermittent areas of erudition well beyond the level of a twelve-year-old. There is also evidence of originality and perhaps even of artistry.

Jordi is fearful of contact with his contemporaries, and this can be understood on many levels, among them his great inexperience in this area.

There is evidence of increasing obsessive defensive maneuvers. This is, however, felt to be a good prognostic sign, since the latter is probably a substitute for his earlier autistic existence.

Diagnosis: At this time deferred.

Prognosis: In view of excellent progress, the future looks relatively bright—we hope.

Recommendation: Discharge from this institution within a year. Jordi should then be ready for formal psychoanalytic treatment while attending an ordinary school. We feel that the latter school must be small and provide for individual understanding and attention.

At the time of discharge we will refer Jordi to one of our list of child psychoanalysts, who may then have a conference with our staff and Jordi's teacher.

The Beginning

Jordi, how do you feel about going to another school?"

"Another school?" he asked, obviously confused. "Will you be there? Will you be there with me, Sally?"

She went on. "Jordi, you don't understand. Do you remember we once talked about more grown-up schools, about high schools and colleges?"

"Yes, I remember, but will you be there, Sally?"

"No, Jordi, I won't be there—but you will learn a great deal more about angles, about history and many interesting things. And there will be other teachers there, and you will meet children your age there too."

"I don't want to go, Sally. I want to stay with you."

"You're not leaving yet, Jordi. It won't be for another six months."

"Do I have to go? Do I have to, Sally? Who will I talk to? Who will tell me I'm Jordi if I get lost—who, Sally?"

He began to cry, and she hugged him to her.

"You won't get lost, Jordi. You're lots better now. Your problem hardly shows anymore—that's why you don't have to stay. You can go to a regular school."

"You mean Lisa can't leave?" he said through his tears.

"No, she can't leave, Jordi. Besides, Jordi, you will have Dr. Mills to talk to. You will see him every day after school."

"Oh, Sally—oh, why did you tell me, why? Now my problems will show—now mine will show."

"Let them show, Jordi, and cry all you like. And, Jordi," she said, "you will visit me. You can come now and then, and I'll come and see you at home every few months. We can talk on the phone, too."

"Everything hurts. Please, please, don't say any more, Sally."
But Sally said much more. They talked and talked about his
departure from the school.

And then only two days remained before Jordi would leave.
Four and a half years had passed since he entered the "ice house."

"Jordi, in two days you will go to your new school, but remember you can visit here."

He suddenly swirled about, faced her, and yelled, "You hate
me, you hate me. You lied, you lied. You never liked me never.
And I hate you, I hate you."

He picked up a blackboard eraser and threw it, shattering the
nearest window.

Then he ran out of the room and out of the building. He just
ran and ran, too dazed to think or watch where he was going.
But he soon found himself on the subway and in the front car of
the Lexington Avenue express.

He rode all over New York and cried most of the time. Then
he thought about Sally and the times gone by. Then he thought
about their talks of the last six months.

When he got back, it was six o'clock, but everybody was still
there. Even his mother and father were there.

Then he saw her, and she said, "Jordi, I'm so glad to see you.
I'm so glad to see you, Jordi."

He looked at her and said, "I came back, I came back. Sally,
I came back to leave."

Little Ralphie
and the Creature

Preface

Some years ago I worked as a psychiatric resident in a northern. New York State hospital.

One late afternoon in midwinter a busload of committed patients was shipped to us from Bellvue. All of them were adults with one exception.

Among them was a boy with whom we could not communicate in any way. He was obviously isolated in his own autistic world. We did not know his name, age, or anything else about him except that he was found lying in the street frozen, starved, and dehydrated. He was brought to Bellvue where he was returned to good physical condition, mainly with gastric tube feedings and intravenous fluid infusions. Psychopharmacological drugs as we know them today did not exist. The tentative Bellvue diagnosis was severe disassociative reaction with catatonic overtones. Our state hospital admission diagnosis was acute schizophrenic reaction—catatonic type.

The boy was tall and gangly and moved about when guided in a stiff, robot-like way. He did not seem completely out of contact nor did he demonstrate the waxy flexibility of complete catatonia. At times he seemed to be responding to auditory hallucinations but we couldn't be sure. As we guided him, he seemed utterly indifferent and compliant. Physical examination was unremarkable.

We estimated his age to be between fifteen and seventeen. A nurse at Bellvue thought she heard him say, "Little Ralphie" and put this name in his accompanying note. She also wrote that he was too young to call him John Doe.

Since the adolescent unit was extremely overcrowded he was sent to the regular male chronic unit. It was felt that he would be safer there than in any acute ward where people were not as "burned out" and resigned and therefore more likely to act out—sometimes violently.

We wrote orders that he should be watched for hydration and nourishment problems and to use a gastric tube if necessary.

In nonmedical terms he seemed to me to stare and move as if he felt himself to be in a swampy, sluggish haze with absolutely no goal in mind.

I thought of Ralphie often through the years and finally decided to write this story about him.

I

The screams and crashing noise and any other sound at all was the last he heard for some time.

And when he left the house, *they* were the last whole people he saw for some time.

He was never going to be hurt again. So he rolled his self into a ball and shrunk it tighter and tighter until it was very small. Then he put it behind his spinal column just above the hip line. From there he started the body going and it walked stiffly like T.V. robots he had seen and headed for the bridge. Klomp, klomp, klomp it went. It was slowly but surely on it's way, away from all noise and people. It was on automatic. So he put the ball self—his self—completely out of awareness as the body took him over the bridge to the city.

———

The body walked over the bridge carrying its blanked-out back-seat passenger around the city for two and a half days.

Nobody noticed the stiff, walking teenage automaton.

But then the body collapsed. For two and a half days it had had no food, water or rest.

In the evening of the third day someone noticed and it was picked up by the police an hour later.

———

He came into awareness enough to feel hands prodding and probing the body he was using. He felt eyes looking it over and noses smelling it and again hands feeling the belly, tapping the chest, hitting the knees and he knew that there was talking. He hadn't turned on the sound of the ears but he could feel the vibrations of the voice sounds.

He turned on the eyes and saw hands and feet and faces—all disconnected—all moving and the mouths talking. But they couldn't see him. No one could see him. He was hidden in his little curled up ball and no matter what they did he knew he would not come out.

How safe and warm he was now.

The body was a necessary connector to the outside dangerous world. It was a vehicle and he was invisible. It was a moving castle, a fort of flesh, a wall between him and all the torture he would never endure again. It was a creature. It was *his* creature!

Let the hands probe. Let the mouths move. Let the feet shuffle. Let them stick needles in the arms and hammer the knees and scratch the soles of the feet.

He was safely removed.

But before he left awareness again he wondered if anyone suspected that a tiny self was living somewhere deep in there and had at last found peace.

The body felt stronger. It felt very strong. In fact he knew that it was ready for its robot walk. But the alien hands and moving mouths didn't know. There were still bottles attached to it by tubes and there were also straps holding it down. He was convinced they were pumping it up with gasoline or maybe gas and electricity. Whatever it was, he knew it didn't need any more. It had enough but they obviously didn't care or didn't know.

The new hands, eyes, and mouths arrived. They looked in the creature's mouth. Perhaps they were looking for him—his self. They looked in the creature's ears with lighted tubes. They talked a lot very loud. He could tell by the vibrations. Then he realized they were trying to figure out if the creature was deaf and if he could talk.

But he couldn't hear and he couldn't talk because he had short circuited him and he would not reconnect to him. He would keep him deaf and dumb so that none of them—none! none!— could find him in his little ball control behind the creature's spine.

The way they rushed and bumped about meant that time was important to them. His world was totally different; there was nothing for him to have to do. Free, he was truly free. Even as he existed, the burdens of existence were no longer his. He was safe from need, safe from wishes, safe from losses, safe from happiness and especially safe from misery.

Through the creature he felt frustration. The frustration was in the air. It wasn't his. It couldn't be! It must have been theirs. Yes, it was their frustration. It was the way they poked, probed, and jabbed the creature. This was more than examining. It was designed to hurt, to punish, but why? Not that he cared. He was safe after all. Then he knew. It was always the same. It was because they couldn't have what they wanted. They wanted to find something, anything, wrong with the body. But they couldn't because there was nothing wrong. So they manufactured frustration—a kind of lingering mood of tension. He knew it well, and now the creature knew it as it felt their pokes and probes and loud voice vibrations and the mouths jabbered away angrily. But he was disconnected from all of it and remained an indifferent bystander.

—◦◦◦—

And then they must have given the creature a powerful injection because self was suddenly fully connected to the eyes and ears. Fortunately *he* remained hidden. Muscle, bone bodily organs— all of the creature's innards continued to separate the small ball, the homunculous, his self from *them*.

But he could not shut them out. The drug—and he assumed it was a drug—transcended his short-circuiting power and made the connections despite the strongest effort on his part to resist. Yes, he could now hear and see them. Their body parts were connected into whole beings. He still managed to keep them hazy—both image and sound—but in large part they came through the haze and somehow they seemed robot-like, wooden and clumsy to him. But it was not enough. He needed to blot them out. Without the straps he could raise the creature's hands to its eyes. But there would still be the ears. He could cover the ears. He could cover the ears but then the eyes would see. And there were the straps, and even without them they, the hazy figures, would surely keep the hands from the eyes and ears.

He could just close the eyes. He tried. But they stayed open. He knew he needed something more subtle and more effective and more controlling—from his self, from the ball within.

He would hear the word, see the faces and he would render them meaningless—just sounds and images meaning nothing—zero.

The words said, "severe disassociative reaction." The words said, "perhaps catatonic." The words said, "severe disassociative reaction with catatonic overtones." He heard the words and saw the faces making them and it all meant nothing.

But a thought came up in his self. Supposing sight and sound were not due to any strong injection. What if they were due to the creature itself. He suddenly became very frightened and wondered if the creature could read his thoughts. If he had to abandon the hiding place he would be vulnerable to all of it again. He must stay. The creature could not make him come out. He screamed out NO! NEVER! NO!

Of course no one heard him. It was all contained within the ball of his curled up self. The creature's mouth hadn't moved at all. This made him feel better. The creature was not in charge.

He was in charge. More important—the separation from the body continued. He felt safer and calm. He was Self after all!

—————

Fifteen days passed but he didn't know it. Time had ceased to have meaning for him. Day and night had meaning for the creature because the creature slept and awoke and had limitations like fatigue. But his separation from the creature made him tireless. He was no longer subject to creature discomforts or, more important, to creature pain. His separation was so complete he needed no sleep. He himself had become the simplest of selves— just an existing entity with its own words and thoughts to build its own cocoon world with, and also its own mind pictures, which he knew were more real than eye pictures and sounds flashed through to him by the creature. Actually he stopped thinking of time as time or as past, present, and future. He thought of it as he experienced his own new existence, and his term for time became "ongoing." Ongoing was neither fast nor slow. It simply *was,* and he and all that he saw in his inner world went on with it.

—————

Their words were meaningful, but he was able to slow up their transmission sufficiently so that they came through as disconnected sounds rather than as words or sentences.

"No identification at all."

"Maybe fifteen!"

"Thin, tall, gangly. I'd say more—seventeen, eighteen."

"Hydrated. OK. Considering the tube feeding, nourishment is fair, too."

"Is he a schiz?"

"I think he has a profound disassociative reaction."

"I think he's catatonic."

"Let's call it that—profound disassociative reaction with catatonic overtones."

"Neurological and physical are OK. E.E.G. and everything else is negative. Simply no organic findings."

"None of the medication worked?"

"Hasn't changed a thing."

"Tried all the strong stuff?"

"All of it. Just slept."

"Ship him to State?"

"If the judge agrees."

"The judge will agree. No place else for him." The voice sighed and said, "Another state hospital adolescent schizophrenic."

⸺◦⸻

On the hospital bus going upstate the creature attacked. It told him that it wanted him to have full vision, full hearing, and regular food.

It started with sandwiches passed around on the bus. Against his will, the creature took one from the attendant's hand and made him glimpse the entire man to whom the outstretched hand was attached.

And then the voice commanded, "Eat It!" But he could see the man's mouth and it hadn't moved at all. And he knew it was the creature's voice. And he also knew that if he obeyed, he would not only lose mastery—through the sandwich, he would reconnect to the outside. Then the creature sniffed the sandwich, and as remote as he was in his little ball he too could smell it— ham and cheese!

"Eat it!" the voice said.

"Throw it out the window!" *he* retorted. And he knew that this was no small matter. There was much more at stake here than a sandwich. Everything was at stake here. Everything! And he made the creature do it. He threw it out the window.

The creature obviously was trying to penetrate his ball of a self, and used loud voices to do it. But he rolled his self tighter and tighter and smaller and smaller, and the effort muted the creature's voice to a harsh whisper so that he could not make out the words. Then the voice was gone.

He felt peaceful again. But the attendant was back. He was giving out second sandwiches to those that wanted them, and bottles of flavored soda drinks. And suddenly the voice boomed out, surprising and shocking him into full awareness. "Take one, fool! Take one or I'll show you what power I have. I'll reconnect. I'll pierce your ball! I'll smash your ball! I'm hungry and thirsty. We will need our strength because where we are going may be worse than the hell we came from."

His thought message to the creature was, Worse for you. Not for me. I'm safe. You can't scare me with your loud voice. I am just a self. I don't need food. I don't need anything.

"Fool!" the voice hissed, "You need me. I need you. Without each other we are both lost. Without a body there is no self. Nowhere to go, Fool!"

But he noted with satisfaction that the creature obeyed and took neither sandwich nor soda and the voice no longer penetrated the globe.

And now the ball had changed into a globe—a globe—a world—his world of which he was the only master.

⊷⊷⊷

And then the bus stopped and self in globe through creature was led off the bus into the cold and then, after a stiff walk, into an overheated place. But he kept the globe at a comfortable temperature and thought with satisfaction that even cold and heat no longer had meaning for the simple, true self he had curled up into.

As their mouths moved at the creature, he noted with comfort that he heard nothing.

Then the wonderful truth came on him. His self would never

grow old, would never be sick and of course would never be hurt. But a sound here and there penetrated the globe and disrupted the insight, and for a terrifying second produced a doubt which he managed to eradicate.

Then as they led the docile creature away, he floated the globe onto an endless ocean. How wonderful to be master of his own universe.

—⊶⊷⊶—

E*at, Fool!"* the voice of the creature commanded again. "Eat and see and hear!"

But he drifted on the ocean, and through the globe which he now made transparent he watched clouds form beautiful shapes and assume various colors. Then he made the globe roll upon a quiet beach and allowed sounds of birds to come through. But they were not those of sea birds, but rather song birds singing light melodic tunes which brought even more tranquility and peace to his self.

"Eat, Fool!" and strangely the creature's voice sounded like a voice out of the past, and this resemblance, though he did not recognize it, erased the ocean, the beach, the birds and their songs, and he could not resurrect them.

But suddenly he had an enormous insight. Why not placate the creature? Let the creature eat. Let the creature see. Indeed, command him to eat. Command him to see.

"Eat!" he commanded the creature. "EAT!"

"Yes," he went on, "Eat and see."

He was gratified—even more—he was comforted. He could do it! He could disassociate and disconnect from the body that was once his, so completely that neither food nor sighted images need reach him. He could haze them out. He could blot them out—totally. The creature could eat, but his self would not. Disconnection was complete and he could do it. He was in charge after all!

As the creature ate, his indifference grew. After all it was not he who was eating. Actually he was no longer even there. He was on his ocean again.

In the distance he saw a boat. There were many little figures in it. They looked familiar. A large wave swamped it. Then they were there in the water shrieking—drowning—and he remained impassive.

The creature ate, and he saw a tremendous shark eat them and the bubble was surrounded by their blood. But none of this was his concern. He felt nothing.

—⚙—

The screams on the ward woke the creature.

But Self was awake all along. He had been sitting in a store of some kind. Other people, all familiar, were sitting in front of him and a large plate glass window. A huge truck suddenly burst through the glass. The noise was horrifying. It was a combination of screams and glass shattering. Limbs, heads, bodies, splinters of glass, impaled abdomens went flying. But he was more than indifferent. He was bored.

The creature thrashed about—an appropriate response to the intermittent screams, laughs, speeches from many private worlds on the ward.

—⚙—

His little tightly rolled self was huge with density. He remembered reading about the Big Bang and how the universe would some day go back to being the size of a tennis ball. But the ball would be the weight of the entire universe since it was the most densely packed molecular structure possible, a ball of almost infinite density. Then it would explode into the spread-out universe again.

He was like that—small and infinitely large, and what made

him large—larger than all of *them,* big as *they* and the creature, too—was the fact that he had the power to freeze them out of his world—out of his existence.

This was the great discovery! His strength, his size, his power had nothing to do with actual size. In fact it was all inversely proportional to physical size. The great discovery was that it was also inversely proportional to need. He was all-big and all-powerful because he had obliterated all need.

—⟨⟨⟩⟩—

Self remained passive, but the creature became increasingly active and in his stiff-gaited way took to exploring.

He discovered that he was in a huge ward of sixty beds. This was connected to a kitchen, a dining hall, a very large day room, a large multiurinal, a nursing station, ten small lock-in rooms, three consultation rooms, a medical treatment room, more than a dozen closets, and several storage and record rooms. There was also a shock room. All of this was connected by corridors and halls of varying diameters. Nearly all doors except the one to the floor—the ward complex—were unlocked. But the door to the ward contained heavy locks to which only hospital employees had keys.

He discovered people and he was extremely sensitive to them and very wary of them. The creature knew that the people observed him—even the men who lay rigidly in their beds never moving, never even blinking, attached to many tubes—even those, and there were eight of them who sat only in corners of rooms and halls, with backs and arms against walls so no one could creep up behind them. Even the giant who sat facing the wall and who got up each hour to face another wall. Even the screamers, the silent screamers—faces contorted because they couldn't let the screams out, the quiet screamers—who never stopped screaming but only in muted tones, and the intermittent explosive screamers—painfully loud, one of whom screamed only the word "fuck" each time he was seized by the attack.

Even the talkers—those who spoke mysterious languages only understood by themselves, those who repeated the same words over and over again; one man said, "Jacky," nothing else, repeatedly, and the people in white called him "Jacky." But some of the other people called "Jacky, Jilly" every time he passed by. Jacky ignored them all. There was one man the people in white called "Fishman" because he would eat only fish. They tried to fool him, but Fishman could always tell and turned down all food but fish, even though they called it fish and flavored it with fish. There were the many little gray men—some were actually tall and thin like the creature himself. It was hard to tell one from the other. They were more like shadows than people. They were always there like endless background music, or not even music— just a gray din filling in space between more substantial people.

They all observed him. He, the creature, knew it. Ralphie was oblivious. And the monitors observed him. The monitors were the women in white and the men in white. But three different men watched him in a different way. They watched him with great hunger in their eyes—their sad but hungry eyes.

———

He knew it was the creature. Floating on the endless sea didn't help. The intrusive voice penetrated stillness. Then he tried to blot it out with his own noise. He started with a low din and graduated to a world-filling, continuous thunder. But the creature pierced sound and stillness of any quality or intensity, this time with shrill words made of sounds like glass breaking.

"I hate this place," the breaking glass said.

"You will have to talk to me," it continued.

"Why?" he asked with a thought.

"Because I will take you back. I will make you feel. I will make you care. I will make you talk—to them—*to them*. I will make you go back."

"I am the self—not you!" Ralphie answered in thought.

"I will call you 'Self!' " the broken glass said. And then in a sudden switch to a booming voice it said, "And you can call me 'Creature'—for now!"

"Creature, enough! Enough! I am shutting you off. You are off and out. As of now you are silent. No voice at all. Silent!"

"I am who I am, Self," Creature boomed, and Self tightened himself into an even smaller ball and knew that he had a problem with Creature even as he rolled out to sea again.

⸺

They were the ghosts. They were not of earth substance. They were all in white and part of a white dimension that had nothing to do with him or his world. They drifted in and around and about, and sometimes disappeared completely, and then were there again drifting and doing their own things in their white misty, hazy world.

But one was intrusive. A voice said that she was Izzabella. Again and again she led the creature into her office and asked him questions—name? age? the past? early childhood? The creature remained mute. Only he and the creature talked and thought.

He thought to the creature, "There was, is, no early childhood."

"Blotted it out?" the creature boomed.

"Was never there," he thought.

"Born in the middle of now?" the creature asked.

"Exactly," Self thought back to the creature.

"But you know you were a baby once," the voice persisted quietly.

"Quiet!" Self ordered.

Creature turned off and Self was now alone on a breezy island in a vast sea—green, all of it green—even the air was green and the smell of it all was green—all in different shades but all green and alive.

And then they were there! Huge sharks, Manta Rays and ill-defined monsters, all with teeth and all of them enraged. And he suddenly didn't feel like Self at all. He was a flake of gold fish food waiting for obliteration.

He must take charge, he told himself. He must think these creatures out of existence. He must clear the sea—*his* sea—of them. But the piece-of-flotsam feeling he had become would not go away even after he saw himself on dry land again.

Creature heard it all.

"I am the bright Angel of Death."

"That's an oxymoron."

"Are you calling me a moron?" the man asked without any emotion at all.

"I am saying that the Angel of Death can't be bright. Death is dark."

"That's where you are wrong," he answered flatly with no affect. The creature watched and heard, and Self gathered his parts together.

The two men sat across from each other on hard stools separated by a long, low wooden table used three times a day to feed thirty people. There were two such tables—empty between meals.

"You get caught in such crap," the first man said, "just because you taught English—you miss the real message." This was said with total lack of emotion and with no voice fluctuation.

"Which is what?" the short, bearded, fat man asked.

"I free people from their wearisome burdens. I open the door to home again. I carry them to sweet nothingness."

"You are even crazier than I am."

"You don't believe me?"

"Believe what?" the short man asked.

"That I have saved people again and again," the tall thin one said in his flat monotone.

"Saved?" the short man asked.

"Saved from life," the monotone answered.

"I think you are delusional."

"And you, what are you?" the thin man asked.

"I am a manic depressive multi suicide and I will soon be out of here again because my own insanity has abated. I am normal again." Tears filled his eyes. "For a while; anyway," he added in almost a whisper.

"You will succeed and I envy you. You will succeed. But I can't do it. I, Frank Wilson, must stay alive and do my work."

"Your work?"

"Yes, to return my sisters and brothers to the peaceful nothingness they were forced to leave. You will do it for yourself. You will end your tortured life and you will be free. You do not need me—the Angel of Light."

"You can go fuck yourself!" the short man screamed, and he got up and walked off in one quick motion, leaving the creature and Frank Wilson staring at each other.

"You need release," Frank said flatly.

The creature did not reply.

"You are young," Frank stated in his flat voice. "You are young and He, the Almighty, awaits you! 'Bring me the blessed ones,' he told me, 'the maimed, defective suffering ones. Bring them to me and to my kingdom of emptiness. Give them transportation through the vehicle of death. The sad sick ones, like you,' he said, 'Frank, bring them to me so that they need not endure years and years of burdensome life!' I do my work as I can and where I can. The insane people in charge here simply do not understand."

The creature did not understand. Self did not care and the creature walked off stiffly.

Later in the day the short, bearded man approached Ralphie and said, "My name is Dave Carney—stay away from that lunatic," and then he walked off.

I'm your doctor," the white-coated one said. The creature sat stiffly and did not reply.

"My name is Izzabella," and then, as an afterthought, "Izabelle Izzabella."

Her voice tickled the creature. There were little bell bubbles in it that made him feel good—yes, actually *feel good* and he wanted to encourage her. He wanted to say a word or to smile or to just move his lips or an eyebrow—only an eyebrow, but Self was in complete control and wouldn't let him budge. They could lead him in and out of offices but Self had otherwise cut him off.

"My friends call me Izz,"—her tinkly tickly voice went on. "Perhaps we can be friends. When you feel like it you call me Izz."

I feel like it. I feel like it, Creature thought. But Self—from his tiny command post—said in thought words to the creature,

"I am in charge—your feelings have no value at all so keep shut—all shut—shut! shut!"

And the impossible happened.

Self slept.

The creature knew because he suddenly felt more of every-thing—the odors on the ward, hunger, the impact of screams—especially curses—the images of the ghost-like, white-dressed people. And then he thought of her voice of bubbles and he walked to her office and hesitated in the hall for a moment.

But Self woke and ordered Creature to return to the day room. Creature was so startled he complied at once.

Self was startled, too.

Could he have actually slept? Creature slept—he knew that

he, Self, needed no sleep. He had no needs at all. But what if he did? And then he knew that Izzabella was dangerous. The creature could use her to force him out of his cocoon. He did not know how, but he knew there was potential danger in a Creature–Izzabella linkage. He also knew that somehow his sleeping was linked to the talk Izzabella had aimed at him through the creature.

Then he had a dreadful idea. Could Creature have put him to sleep? Did Creature have that ability? If so, what other powers did he have? But he rolled himself tighter and squeezed this kind of worry out of awareness and existence.

And he made sure that he was in total charge each time Izzabella made rounds. He made sure that the creature responded in no way at all to her questions or show of interest.

However, Creature had other ideas.

II

At first their sessions were almost totally unproductive because Ralphie said nothing. Ralphie (and the entire staff called him by that name after a few days) made grunting and wheezing sounds but no words at all came out.

Izz knew that Ralphie was not neurologically impaired. But when Ralphie tried to communicate he seemed to imitate the most serious kinds of spastic disorders. His face became brick red and contorted with effort. Pencil and paper produced jagged unintelligible scribbling. She thought of an Amytal interview but decided that in the long run he would resent it and it would be counterproductive.

Izz guessed that she was witnessing a powerful struggle, possibly between conflicting forces, but had no evidence to support that theory. She noted that when attempts to communicate ceased, Ralphie's face returned to its composed, "sweet-looking" contours.

But after several sessions, Self realized that he hated to be called Ralphie and could not understand why they all used that name. And he immediately caught himself. He must hate nothing at all. He must feel nothing at all. He must care nothing at all. They could call *him* Ralphie or anything else. He cared nothing about *him*. There was no *him*. There was only his self—his well hidden, tiny, densely packed molecular and impenetrable self—that no one, no one, no one could reach—not even the softest-voiced, tinkling-voiced, gentlest-voiced, and softest-looking of any of *them* or anyone else. No one could reach him! He was safe! And he wasn't bored. He had his lives to live.

Tiny red ants scurried up and back, milking aphids, stirring twigs and leaves, very busy and happy to be alive and safe and cozy and in a wonderful world—a large potted rubber plant.

And he was one of them. He was small and his family was too small for people to see. They were almost microscopic. This large rubber plant was one of several but they didn't know that. They were much too small to climb up the sides of the pot—which were very high, steep, and smooth. They seldom got up to more than a few inches on the plant trunk. Their lives were spent in the earth itself and in a very small section of the total container. He loved to be there. This was his family. They loved him and accepted him. No one ever faulted him. In fact, no one even thought in those terms. Faults simply did not exist.

But he had a secret—one from another place and time—a terrible secret, and periodically it would start to drown him in sadness. Sometimes his mood would turn to black despair. And he would escape the despair through a magical route.

And he was in the ocean. He was a whale, an enormous whale and he was one of a family of whales. They lived in a deep, serene, endless ocean but more important—they lived in a sea of sound—their own sounds mostly. Their smooth pearly skins pulled tightly over their enormous frames functioned as the largest living eardrums and amplifiers in the universe. And they knew all the sound channels of the ocean connecting all the oceans and bays of the world. It was these connecting sound channels that made their ocean endless, and they could talk to relatives and friends all over the world—and they did.

All whales were friends. No matter distance—they heard each other. They understood each other. There were no misunderstandings, no fights—ever! And they cared. Yes, they cared!

And so their sounds were beautiful symphonies of acceptance and understanding.

There were bloody wars in the oceans but only peace prevailed in the boundless ocean of sound.

And now he was Ralphie again—Ralphie and the creature.

Somehow he had come to think of himself by that silly name—
Ralphie—and someone was calling his name.

It was the creature and he was demanding food. Ralphie let
him eat. It was easier and it really didn't matter anyway. He knew
that he was in charge. So he let Creature go into the dining room
and eat.

He had no way of knowing and would not have cared anyway
that the people in white saw this as excellent progress—especially
Izz.

—⸺⟊⟆⸺—

The office of Izz. Creature sits and says nothing. Izz talks. Creature is mute. He hears nothing. Ralphie is away. Creature cannot
contact him. But he sees her mouth move. He tries to answer—
to respond to words he cannot hear. He screams inward to Ralphie—but he is away. "Turn ears on!" he screams. But Ralphie
is away. He tries to respond anyway. His mouth moves. No voice
comes out. His mouth makes what looks like random grotesque
contortions. But even this pleases Izz. She smiles. Creature
smiles—but it is not a smile that shows. It is a twisted "funny
face"—not unlike a Popeye cartoon.

Tim, and that's the ant name Self uses, is watching his sister
Louise. She is on a very low leaf of the plant. Really not a leaf
at all. A bud, an almost invisible bit of a bud and it is a very shaky
dead bud. Tim is terrified. Liz may fall off.

Izz talks in a loud voice.

The bud Liz is on trembles. Tim motions her to come down.

Creature is oblivious to the smile—he only sees her mouth
move and he moves his in spastic, non-voice contortions. Izz
continues to talk loud, louder.

As the bud falls, Tim vanishes and George, Self's whale name,
is gliding through a deep but light green sea and warm sound is
everywhere.

Izz has stopped talking. Creature stiffly makes his way back to
the day room.

Don't go into the cove!" he told them.

"Why not?" they asked.

"Stay in our open sea," he pleaded.

"But we can rest and play in the cove."

"The water is still and quiet," one of them said.

"Please, please—not in the cove," he begged.

No! He would not let Creature go into her room. He must not go in. He must not!

Creature said that he wanted to see her and then he pleaded. Then he demanded.

Ralphie felt the tug of the sea. He felt the tug of the rubber plant. But he resisted. He had to hold on to Creature.

"Why?" Creature asked.

Ralphie would not answer.

He did not know why in words or anything that resembled logic.

But he did know that her room was a threat to the contracted self he had become. He knew in the most concentrated part of his "molecular being" that human contact led to loss and to unbearable pain. But this knowing was not of a thinking or verbal kind. He could not verbalize this to himself, let alone to Creature. He just knew. And he also knew that it was imperative to sustain his hold over Creature—*imperative*—and this word he did know. And so he issued the command, "No!" and into the command he concentrated the full force—the totality of what he came to think of as his "molecular self," and Creature froze.

Regression!"

Creature heard this word over and over again and others also.

"Catatonic stupor, this time."

"What kicked it off?"

"Give him E.C.T.?"

"No," the tinkly voice went on, "we will wait." And then the tinkly voice went on, "I felt he was going to talk. He tried so hard. And then he wouldn't come into the office."

"Maybe that was it. Maybe he was about to talk and became terrified. This freeze-up instead."

"Maybe," she said.

"Amytal?"

"No," she said. And they started the tube feedings again.

Sometime during the night Creature felt a light, very tentative, almost feather-like touch on his forehead.

But he couldn't move. He was locked in place on the bed by Ralphie, whose control had become total.

The touch was now heavier—the tentative quality was gone. And now there was a kiss on the forehead—not unpleasant. But Creature's eyes staring straight ahead now peered into the man's eyes and felt his prickly beard on his face.

Creature shouted inwardly—"Ralphie! Self!" But there was no answer. It was as if there was no Self. It was as if Creature himself was the only self. But he was a totally paralyzed self.

Then the man got into the bed and hugged Ralphie and gently kissed him on the forehead. Then he left.

Creature wept without tears and without knowing why he wept. But he cried for almost an hour before he fell into a deep, almost comatose-like sleep.

George warned them. "Stay out of the coves," he sang to them in that mournful but beautiful whale sound. "Stay away from them!" he warned. They listened and they complied with his wishes. It was rare that they were warned about anything at all. They were almost never frightened. They were, after all, the largest living beings on the planet. And they were peaceful—so peaceful that it was almost impossible for them to believe living creatures existed who could want to hurt them.

But George was different in some way. He knew it and he knew that they knew it. One of the things that made him different was his sudden disappearances and reappearances. He also seemed to know much more about *them* than any of his fellow whales knew.

And George was frightened of *them* and at times he was very sad because he also knew that *they* always seemed to win out. What if his great-sized brothers and sisters got too close to *them*— to people—when he was away?

◄━━∪▐━━►

Tim's father, William, was a master builder. This meant that his mind designs, which they could all follow without verbal direction, always came out useful, cozy, and warm. Their new home was being done with meticulous care. His mother, Tina, had great taste. Their little house and garden would be something the whole family had dreamed of for a long time. Everyone helped—at least a dozen friends—all of them exceedingly capable and full of energy. They did not need a leader or coordinator of any kind. They simply worked together, tuned into the central theme of their goal, and William's design was spontaneously co-ordinated. From a great distance—as from the lowest plant leaf— they would have looked like one whole workman. But actually they were a team of many cooperative and generous ants. And so the little mound house went up in no time at all—in an ant's month or so, which was a human minute or two. These last thoughts about time had been there in Tim's mind and he knew that they did not belong. In fact all kinds of time comparisons would intrude at odd moments and disturb the contentment he felt. These peculiar "*time terms,*" and one of them was "ongoing," came from outside himself and could be frightening. Fortunately they were fleeting, and the immediate business at hand almost always took over and saved him from prolonged disquietude and unhappiness.

The house was exactly the kind he liked—many little chambers with storehouses for food and repairing materials. There were courtyards here and there for grazing aphids and several large halls for family breakfasts. There was a still larger hall for gatherings of friends and visitors, who sometimes stayed over in one of the chambers. And Tim had his very own library—a small room and desk surrounded by many tiny but thick volumes. *Tiny by human standards*—this thought intruded and he knocked it out of awareness quickly before it could take hold and spoil things. And the main thought that knocked out the intrusive offender was that this house and its replenishing stored material would go on and on—forever, forever?

—————

Creature could hear perfectly, but what he heard filled him with dread.

E!C!T! This is what the small white crowd around the bed were saying. He knew what it meant.

It was a torture sentence.

In his wanderings he saw it done.

E.C.T. was electrocution! It was a kind of dying without death so that the horrible process could be done again and again.

He had seen the victims held down, be electrocuted, and then rise up against the straps as they convulsed and frothed at the mouth, and the agonizing scream tore out of them and they turned blue and even black until they finally breathed again ready for still another execution the next day.

Each patient's bed became the treatment center, and it was not lost on Creature that this spectator activity was a warning to others to behave. And Self was not behaving. He could not be contacted. Perhaps he was dead and had taken his control of

Creature's body with him into death. Creature was terrified that his bed would become an electric torture center as so many others did. He called out into the depths of Self to save them. But his inner voice echoed back, not having made contact with anything or anybody at all. He was an empty creature after all, but he wept internally and in a way his tears filled his emptiness.

It was the voice of Izz, "No!"

Before the "No!" there had been a discussion. There were half a dozen of them and the consensus was "E.C.T." But Dr. Izzabella dissented. In fact her "No!" was the loudest, the most impassioned. The others backed off, not from lack of authority or a changed opinion—they simply didn't care as much as she did. Creature knew this—without verbalizing it, he knew all this. Through their tone, the conversation and its nuances communicated the E.C.T. meaning to him even more than the words themselves.

He heard words that he had heard before and they had dire connotations, even if he didn't understand them exactly. "Catatonic stupor"; "Regression"; "Tube Feedings"; "No Waxy Flexibility"; "stiff as a Board"; "E.C.T.! E.C.T.! E.C.T.!"

He knew what the letters E.C.T. meant and they terrified him. But most important it was the anti-E.C.T. stand of Dr. Izzabella that reached deeper than the rest, and even warmed the chilled void in him to some extent. This stand of hers and its effect remained recorded in him.

<hr />

The plant world was not an even terrain or even climate. The tiny ants could discern great variations in moisture, temperature, and topography in different locations just millimeters apart. For ants that small, little rises in the ground were seen as mountainous areas. In fact, there were very few entirely flat areas. But there were large deserts and many lakes, rivers, and oceans. Tim knew this, and of course he knew about the large trench in the earth and tributary trenches that ran from this central one. This rent in the ground filled with water periodically, and then the water would gradually go down and then fill up again. This tidal rise and fall watered the tributaries and followed a regular schedule with considerable consistency. Minute seepage from the central source kept the plant and everything in the Pot World alive.

Tim and his family lived far away from the ocean in a relatively dry region. But he was afraid that they might somehow wander into an area of total dryness—a desert—and not make it back on time. He also had peculiar thoughts of the waterways overflowing and flooding all of them—even the entire world. It was as if this had happened before—some knowledge he had from a different time and place and being.

But George swam in the deepest oceans and could come up from the depths, soaring out of the water into the air and then diving back into the depths again and then gliding along with the others over vast distances.

And he and scores of his relatives were on their way, talk-whistling all the time, to the great ocean-concert center of the central ocean of the world. They were bathed in sound constantly, and their instant understanding made them feel as if they composed one whole being—one consciousness. George's sense of belonging, of understanding, of being understood, and the peace and comfort this brought, filled his entire being.

But their sounds contributed much more than communication. They were building a melodic ambiance. The confluence of fugues, melody, themes, phrases, rhythms, all coming from various groups, was producing a majestic, symphonic cathedral which moved with them as large groups converged in the center of the central sea. Beams of sunlight produced a translucent ceiling; and sound, water, air, sky, and moving whales provided a perfectly blended unity.

Their journey was slow, so that a perfect harmonious blending could take place as each group of whales made its contribution to the symphonic world of sound. And George swam in the middle, and as they approached the center of the ocean, the center of the great confluence, time slowed and then stood still.

Creature couldn't move. He slipped in and out of various levels of consciousness. At times his awareness was nil. At other times he was in a heavy haze. And there were also brief moments of extremely sharp, acute awareness during which his perceptions of everything around him were magnified and sharply delineated.

His mind produced no complete thoughts—only fragments—disconnected words now and then and thought pictures which were like half dreams. The foci of these inner visions were usually soft and diffuse. And there were disconnected fragment visions of oceans, beaches, tiny ants, and strange but melodic sounds—none of which connected or made any sense.

But through it all and superimposed upon it all, and even coming through his unconsciousness to him, was her voice. And he would remember her words—always.

She spoke slowly and paused a great deal. But she spoke enough so that he knew she was there much of the time of his consciousness and unconsciousness. He also knew there were long periods when she was not there. And her absence filled him with more than her presence. It produced a feeling in him—something that had become almost extinct. The feeling was longing. He could not define it; nor did he know that he longed for her. But that is what it was. He longed for her. It was a very subtle, minimal longing, but it was the beginning of wanting something.

"I am here," she said.

"I think you hear me."

"I will be here several times a day—almost every day."

"One day we will talk. Until then I'll sit with you. I just want you to know I will wait."

And in a moment of awareness a terrible thought flashed through his mind—Ralphie might not come back if she stayed with him. And yet there was the longing and the beginning of wanting. Creature wanted her to stay.

After half an hour she said she would come back the next day, and she did.

"I'm here." She greeted him.

After a long pause and with considerable hesitancy, she spoke.

"I think you wanted to talk to me—that you did and you didn't, and this made you feel pulled apart and afraid. But I will wait."

Creature did not respond but suddenly Ralphie did. He was neither George nor Tim—only Self—and he was on full alert as Creature stirred slightly.

Ongoing: But Creature remained comatose.
               Self, Ralphie was in charge.

The voice of bubbles was not safe. It provided a stimulation unlike any other. And the most stimulating aspect of it was not the voice at all. It was the presence attached to the voice, and that presence made itself most apparent when she was silent. But even then the memory and feel of the bubbles remained. When she left he quickly left, too. It was the fastest way to rid himself of the residual effects of her presence.

Tim and his sister, Louise, milked the aphids for a while and then Tim went into the library and sat surrounded by the shelves of books. There was great comfort in the air. Even the musty smell of books made it just right. It was more than comfort or peace or safety. What it mainly was, was at-homeness. In this place he was at home with himself.

Tim looked over some books Louise had suggested he read. She was older than him and sometimes he believed she had read just about anything worthwhile ever written. Yes, Louise was very smart, one of the smartest ants he had ever met.

Everyone who knew her admired her. But they also liked him. Yes they did. He knew they did. They liked him, he reassured himself; but the library now felt closed in—tight.

George and the others were returning from the great musical conclave. They were completely at peace and full of joy—the result of the magnificent symphonic construct they had created. He knew that what had sounded like random notes were always there waiting to be put together in a harmonious blend. They had made that blend, and in so doing had brought to life a music that had always been there in the first place—waiting to come together and to be released as a creative unity. Satisfaction was enormous and more filling than the air they breathed or food they ate. Having shared in the birth and realization of cooperative production, they were all bonded forever. George felt this. Words, thoughts, intellectual understanding would have been superfluous.

—————

William made a little boat out of a minute twig and the four family—that's how Tim thought of William, Tina, Louise, and himself, as the "four family"—went boating on the small lake near their home. It was a lot of fun as they all used their legs to row and steer the boat. Tim promised himself to bring along some fishing equipment next time they went, because he could see an occasional ameba and paramecium in the water. He even saw a few large daphnia which would be a real challenge for ants so small.

When they got home some of their extended family was there and everyone was in a very good mood. They ate at a long table (in human terms only a few millimeters long) which was loaded with food they had all gathered. Much of it had been fished from lakes in the area—parameceum and several species of daphnia, as well as algae and vegetation dropped by the rubber plant.

"Don't overeat," William said to Tim.

William could be a worrier. When they were on the boat he kept a constant vigil, making sure that they wouldn't capsize and that the weather remained good. But Tim and the rest of the family understood this and it seldom spoiled their good time.

"Overeat" seemed funny to Tim. This was really an unnecessary worry. Tim never overate. He was always trying to gain weight and Tina was ever concerned that he did not eat enough. It was William himself who nearly always ate too much and then complained of indigestion. Louise had no problem with weight. As with most other things, Louise had no problems.

But what problems any of them had did not interfere with their happiness or their very tight closeness to each other. In fact they were so close they really felt like a single unit. Therefore anyone's problem was everyone's problem. Anyone's success was everyone's success. This kind of closeness went way beyond loyalty.

Some friends came over and they were invited to eat too, so they all moved the food outside and dinner turned into a wonderful picnic, which attracted some neighbors and ants just passing by. It broke up when rain started to fall in very heavy torrents. This made Tim very anxious, and again gave him a peculiar reaction as if from another time and place. A very strange picture passed through his mind. It was of a big upended lake pouring down in torrents over the whole world. In a different consciousness he would have recognized it as a bucket of water. But his immediate well-being required him not to recognize it. And so he felt anxious and strange and almost wanted to warn them all. Instead, everyone went home as Tim and the rest of the four family went into their house, which was so tight and cozy Tim felt better and put everything weird out of awareness.

⟞⟝

The two men without awareness of each other approached his bed at the same time. One of them began to get into his bed. The other man, Frank Wilson, pulled the man from the bed and slapped him across the face. The man stepped aside, weeping, and said, "I only wanted to love him." Wilson ignored him and put his own face close up to Ralphie's ear.

"You won't have to suffer any more," he said. There was no response from the bed.

"I heard your plea and the good Lord has heard your prayer. I am a servant of the Lord. He said, 'Frank, you are my Angel of Light. Bring him to me as you have the others. His suffering must end!' Child—be happy—your time has come at last. *This* is the Lord's command!"

He carefully placed a pillow over Ralphie's face and he said,

"Be not afraid my child. We will go through a dark tunnel but we will quickly arrive at the valley of light, and from there it is only a short journey to His hand and eternal peace."

He gently but firmly applied pressure to the pillow.

There was no perceptive response from the inert rigid body.

But Creature heard Frank's voice and he felt the pillow on his face and he understood the message, and he was catapulted into full conscious awareness and terrible agony because he could not budge.

Paralysis! Panic! Pleas to Self for release were silently screamed inward. These were conveyed to the inner empty cavern in which Self could not or would not be found. He had the fleeting thought that Self was dead; that only he, Creature, was left. But his paralysis instantly convinced him otherwise. He was still in Self's lock.

And then, when he felt his chest would burst and he did see the white light, he made the greatest effort in his life and broke through to Self. The steamroller effect of his enormous effort gave Self no chance for heroic resistance. With the effort, a scream—that of a severely tortured, wounded creature—tore out of him and this time it was heard by all.

In this moment Self and Creature were one.

The enormous energy which paralyzed and held him rigid exploded into a violent outburst. It would by any ordinary logic be impossible to believe that one human being, and a relatively frail one, could contain so much explosive steam. The ordinary outlet for this pent-up emotion, and so much of it, appeared to be rage— the mouth and it's continuous scream was simply not enough. It was as if the ocean were attempting to empty itself through a hose nozzle. Thus the explosion soon involved his entire body, which quickly went into a formidable kind of seizure expressed through utterly wild and violent movement. In those moments his destructive strength was monumental. The outpouring of pent-up emotion through continuous screams and body movement was enormous, having been stored for weeks. It was, in fact, a kind of human atom explosion, and a most fearful sight.

At first he seemed to convulse, but then the convulsion transformed itself into gross and extremely powerful body movement so that he easily broke the straps that held him. Then he rose from his bed and as he ran helter-skelter about the ward, tubes were pulled out of his arms and bottles to which they were attached crashed onto the floor. He hurled himself against beds and walls like a violent, unseeing, primitive force and smashed patients, who had also left their beds, with his fists. His eyes were glazed and his movement seemed to be without organization or objective, but he grabbed a stool that he tripped over and smashed attendants and nurses who entered the ward.

One young attendant whispered to himself, "This is what I always thought going crazy was all about."

Several attendants tried to hold him but he kicked, beat, and clawed his way out of their grip several times.

There was an amazing amount of blood, screams, and general chaos because now at least half a dozen other patients were screaming and running about, flailing at all who came near them. But none exhibited his strength or violence, and his terrible scream was easily heard as it transcended all other noise. The scream had a primitive, guttural, animal quality: There was also terrible anguish in it. Yes, it conveyed anguish and this was intensely human. This juxtaposition of animal rage and human anguish produced a reaction of horror in all those present and intact enough to respond appropriately. But in Dr. Izzabella more than anything else it produced pity and sympathy.

And then, just as it had begun, it abruptly stopped as he collapsed on the floor from exhaustion. Only then were they able to inject him with a strong sedative. The injection was unnecessary. He was obviously unconscious. But the shot was given at least in part out of fear, anger, and frustration at having been unable to contain him.

After they had placed him on his bed his stupor seemed more profound than ever; but physical examination revealed no abnormality whatsoever.

They had no way of knowing that a fierce battle raged within the inert body.

The split had seemingly been reestablished and Self attempted to join his family of whales. But Creature blocked his exit.

With increasing horror Self realized that Creature might be in control.

At first he simply attempted to go. When he couldn't make it happen, he tried to picture the sea and to place himself in a globe on its currents. But that didn't work either.

He commanded Creature—to no avail.

Then he pleaded with him—also to no avail.

Then he used manipulation laced with terror and truth. "I feel we will die," he said. "I must be with them." This reached Creature. It didn't frighten him. It filled him with pity and he let go, and George swam and sang in the ocean.

III

Dr. Izzabella's notes:

Today Ralphie went into catatonic excitement. I've heard that the two most dangerous violent reactions are catatonic excitement and epileptic psychomotor equivalents. However this reaction went quite beyond anything I ever imagined. It was terrifying.

This kind of uncontrollable, violent acting out well describes the word "berserk." Are we all capable of this kind of undifferentiated explosive rage—this total wildness?

He smashed everything in his vicinity. Several patients and attendants were knocked to the ground bleeding. Three required sutures. Furniture was smashed. People could not get out of his way fast enough, and throughout the whole thing he kept screaming this awful, blood-curdling, wrenching, painful sound.

It took seven attendants to catch and hold him so that he could be sedated. And then he collapsed—from exhaustion rather than sedation.

I find myself to be more sympathetic and more challenged than ever. When he screamed I found myself weeping. I am not tough. Several people see his reaction as the height of regression, and there was more talk of E.C.T. But I view this as a possible breakthrough. However, I'm concerned about catatonic exhaust which is, of course, life threatening.

Doesn't this reaction release enormous pent-up rage? If it does, shouldn't this be relieving? If so wouldn't this be appropriately viewed as progress, even though the symptom is potentially destructive and frightening?

The people here evaluate everything on a symptomatic clinical level. My teachers at the psychoanalytic institute see it all in psychodynamic terms. They see E.C.T. as valuable and necessary when life is threatened—such as in suicidal depression. I'm sure they feel the same about catatonic exhaust, which can go on to cessation of all bodily function and death. But they also feel that E.C.T. can destroy a successful and long-term psychotherapeutic change and even a cure. It must certainly disturb the relationship (transference) between patient and doctor.

In any case, I shall continue to sit with him. *But* I must be careful of countertransference. My feeling for him must not result in withholding life-saving treatment. There's a narrow line here and both of us seem to be walking it.

Dr. Izzabella's notes:

I think I've convinced Dr. Brenan (now my supervisor here) that he is in no immediate danger or potentially violent now. Truth is I'm frightened. Am I doing the right thing in withholding E.C.T.? Can he go into excitement again or even worse, exhaust? What makes it all so much more difficult is that I have no history at all on him. I'm tempted to give him an Amytal interview. Brenan encourages it. He says that a few cc's injected I.V., and he will tell much about himself and then have no memory of having said anything at all. There's something sneaky about this. Teachers at the institute feel this kind of intervention is destructive in the long run. They feel that it disregards and even violates the patient's necessary defences. If he needs to be mute he must not be forced to talk.

The issue came up in my own analysis with Nat Harris. Dr. Harris feels that I am going at this too hard. Maybe. Perhaps the patient does remind me of my brother Pete. Of course, I'm aware of countertransference. I'm more than a little aware that I'm spending more than half my time on Ralphie and less than half on about twenty-five other patents.

But I feel okay about this. Nat Harris says that understanding one patient well can teach us more than knowing one hundred people superficially. But truth is, I don't understand Ralphie at all. Nevertheless my feeling for him is strong. Is this maternal? Is it because we lost Pete when he was about the same age? Is it both? Is it neither? He looks a little like Pete—or is this my imagination—or wish—to somehow make it up to Pete, because I was kind of distant from him when he was alive and we could have been friends as well as sister and brother?

—————

He felt the tug. As big and strong as he was, he felt the pull. And now it was becoming irresistible. The sea was no longer calm. It became increasingly turbulent. He was no longer a part of a family of whales. He was alone, and the ocean heaved and tossed him about and then ejected him as if he were a small piece of flotsam.

And then he was his tightly wound ball of a self again—safe behind Creature's spine. But he wasn't safe. The ball started to unravel.

Creature was in charge and then he, Self lost consciousness and for the moment succeeded in vanishing into nothingness.

But Creature was now fully conscious.

And Dr. Izzabella was there.

"No E.C.T.," he said. His voice was low and the tone somewhat flat. But there was no evidence of struggle in getting out the words.

"No E.C.T.," she replied.

Then they said nothing. She made a conscious effort to say nothing. The urge to ask questions, to encourage more speech, to show pleasure, was enormous. But she kept quiet and when she left she made sure that his restraints and intravenous tubes were all removed.

—————

Creature resumed eating in the dining room and wandering about. He walked slowly but the robot-like gait was gone.

But he was very apprehensive—always on the lookout for Frank Wilson, the bright Angel of Death, and waiting for the certain return of Self.

The fear of their return was particularly harrowing when he went to sleep. At first he tried to stay awake in case an attack came. But this was impossible, and he was grateful to get up each morning intact having had visitations from neither Frank nor Self.

Then he searched for Frank. If he could locate him he would feel safer. But he could find him nowhere.

He did not attempt to find Self. He felt that this search might be all too fruitful. He tried as much as possible to keep thoughts of Self out of consciousness. But this didn't always work and there were times when fragments of dreams involved both Self and Frank.

Doctor Izzabella visited him every day and sometimes several times a day, but they did not speak and as yet he did not return to the treatment room.

—◦◦◦—

The voice woke him at four in the morning.

At first it repeated his name continuously at five-second intervals and this frightened him into near rigidity. But he struggled to keep moving and he thrashed in the bed.

Self then repeated his name, this time in a rat-a-tat-tat machine-gun burst, and tears ran down Creature's cheeks.

"You thought I was gone," Self whispered.

Hopelessness replaced dread. He felt defeated. But then for the first time a peculiar thought, a completely new concept, entered his head.

He was crazy. He, Creature, was crazy. That Self was there, that he was always in charge, that he existed at all—none of this was verbalized, but it surely meant that he, Creature, was crazy or a fleeting thought that he couldn't quite hold on to—Self was crazy because Creature was there. He felt the craziness. The feeling lasted only a moment. But it had been there. He had a feeling—a real feeling.

And there was more.

This possibility of being crazy did not last. But it reached him out of terror and hopelessness. Because if his problem was only a matter of being crazy, then he was human after all. It meant he was connected—to people. It meant there was hope. Even crazy people *lived*. Even crazy people got well.

These insightful feelings continued without words. But they were strong enough to produce another feeling, one he had totally forgotten—a feeling that had been effectively obliterated, a feeling that now was born again. The feeling was a small, exceedingly mild, only fleeting but quite real surge of happiness. Yes, the idea of being crazy was sufficiently human and real so that it produced hope and happiness—however subtle, small, and short lived.

⟶◦⟵

Did you think I was gone?"

"I could move without you," Creature answered.

"That is all you can do—move—because that is all you are—a vehicle—a litter—a thing—a creature—and even to move you need me."

"I feel."

"You feel?"

"I had a feeling."

"What feeling?"

"That I am crazy."

"You are crazy!"

"Maybe it's you who are crazy."

"You are my invention."

"No. You are my invention."

"You are too much of a fool to invent me," Self hissed.

The idea that he was not crazy immediately depressed him. He did not recognize depression as a feeling, but rather as a never-ending vacuum—empty hopelessness—and yet, unknown to him, it was a feeling.

"I am crazy!" he said to Self.

"*That* is your feeling?" Self asked contemptuously.

Creature did not answer.

Self went on.

"I used to be afraid of you. Now you are afraid of me. You will always be uncertain. There is no way you can know when I will be here—to wake you—to command you."

Creature stiffened. Self went on.

"Did you think I was gone—lost at sea, buried in a pile of sand? Did you really think you were left in charge? Who do you think you are? What do you think you are? Who do you think is whose invention? Did you think I would ever let you get me tortured all over again?"

These last statements were made in a slow, quiet, flat monotone. This lack of affect produced considerable menace, and Creature struggled against stiffening which he knew would lead to board-like rigidity.

To his amazement his struggle succeeded.

"I can move," he said out loud. He got off the bed to demonstrate. Yes, despite Self's presence he walked up and back in front of the bed. He swung his arms and said, "I can move," several times with a bit more affect than he had mustered up to that point.

When he went back to bed, Self was no longer there.

He told William that he was afraid, and then he said a strange thing.

"Beware of the coves!"

William didn't understand this at all.

Tim hardly noticed *his* mistake. He went on to say that he had thoughts of the whole world drying up and everyone dying—everyone—even the great provider—the rubber plant itself.

William reassured him, saying that ants had heard that for millennia; eventually it could happen but certainly not in their lifetime.

But Tim felt uneasy. Information from elsewhere intruded itself in the form of anxiety and so he disassociated himself.

As George, he was in the connected oceans of the world—the absolute antithesis of a dried-up, dead, ant world.

But then he told his friends to stay out of the coves and this brought anxiety, disassociation, and escape to the ball self in back of creature's spine from which the inner dialogue resumed.

"You thought I was gone."

Creature did not answer.

"I made you up."

Creature said nothing.

"You don't know who you are, where you came from or where you are or where you are going—nothing—you know nothing at all."

"I know that you are afraid," Creature replied quietly.

"Afraid! What have I to be afraid of? I'm safe where I am. I can't get hurt—not ever again—nothing can hurt me!"

"You are in pain now," Creature said, and added, "you are afraid."

"You cannot drag me into her office."

"Is that what you want?" Creature asked.

"No! It is you who want it. I know what you think before you think it. You are a robot—nothing else—my invention—you don't even know where you came from. There's nothing you know—nothing at all. I am the Self, the substance, our world, my worlds. You know nothing of my worlds—nothing. Where do you think I go when I'm not here?"

"Without me there is no place you can go. Without me you do not exist. If I stop being you stop being!"

Then Creature hit himself in the nose—hard—several times, until blood flowed down his face. Then, using his nails, he scratched his legs, deep until blood flowed down his legs.

"This blood is real blood," he said, and he wiped the blood all over his hands and face.

Then he screamed out loud.

"I'm real! I'm real!" and continued to scream as he bathed his hands in his own blood and felt so much better for it.

"There is no self without a body," he said as an attendant gave him a sedative shot.

"Hallucinating," the attendant told the nurse on duty. But neither Creature nor Self heard. Ralphie was asleep.

—————

I know you really want to see her." Creature argued.

"Silence!" Self ordered.

"You can't silence me!" Creature thundered.

This time Self responded in a reasonable, not quite patronizing manner.

"You saw what happened the last time you went in to see her. You became stiff as cardboard—paralyzed—in a stupor. This time they will give you shock treatments. They will electrocute you."

"Us!" Creature screamed at him.

"You are stupid!" Self screamed back. "I am not physical. I create and become and go and I'm safe. *You* are the body. *You* will be burned—you can't leave."

"You are the fool!" Creature said quietly. "She would never permit E.C.T." He knew that.

"You can't trust her or anyone or anything—not in this world." Now Self was almost pleading.

"If I die," Creature said quietly, "you will be buried with me. Your trips will stop. Everything will stop. You know it stops when people die—all of it stops."

Self rolled himself tighter and said nothing.

After twenty minutes passed Creature said, "I like her voice."

—————

Alone" he said.

"Yes, we are alone—the two of us here." Izzabella said this as gently as she could.

"Me—alone." he said flatly.

"I'm here with you," she answered.

"Self is gone."

"You are here," she said.

He did not reply.

They sat silently for half an hour and then he returned to the ward.

He walked about easily. He was not stiff. There was no sign at all of spasticity. He was somehow freer, easier, lighter. There was no sign of Self.

When he ate dinner that evening he ate well.

That night Self said, "She didn't understand you." Creature did not answer.

"She thought you were lonely."

"I am lonely," Creature replied.

"She did not know it was me—Self—her little Ralphie who was missing. You told her but she didn't understand."

Creature said nothing, but a heaviness began to fill his chest.

"Maybe she is a fool," Self went on. "You must listen to me. Do not go back. We are alright as we are. Don't let any of them in."

"You are afraid," Creature said.

"I have nothing to fear. I am unreachable. I can leave and no one can follow, no one, no one, no one." Then he was gone but the words "no one" stayed on in Creature's head, repeating themselves over and over again most of the night.

———

He thought about his difficulty finding words and sentences with which to speak to her. He knew without thinking that this was connected to Self's absence, and the words "no one" repeated themselves intrusively and he couldn't stop them. "Self is gone," he said.

But perhaps it was more than Self having the words. He could feel that it was more than Self owning and storing language. Self had the power to block anything out. Self was willful. Self was obstinate. Self could stand in the way between Creature and anything. Like the sandwich on the bus. Self could stand in the way of speech. But eventually Creature did eat. Was it only because Self knew that he would die with Creature without food? Or was it because Creature could break through Self's barricade?

"Alone," he said several times, and then he left.

Dr. Izzabella's notes:

He came in on his own. Surely this indicates enormous motivation. To break through his autistic encapsulation, his severe inhibition, means coming through a great struggle. I think he has decided that I'm a friend or at least not an enemy, and this can make all the difference. I must be careful not to push in any way at all though I have a great temptation to ask all kinds of questions.

Of course his verbal production was very limited, but the few words he said came through smoothly and I think I could detect a little bit of affect, or am I wishful-thinking? I must keep my optimism limited, but I do feel more hopeful and right in my decision to hold back on E.C.T.

Am I being too optimistic? Am I too involved—"countertransference"? His voice is rather mechanical—sounds as if it comes from an empty chamber—an echo feel to it. Does this association of mine mean that I feel he is empty? No! I don't believe it. His inner world and feelings may or may not be rich—but he is not empty.

Dr. Brenan says, "Hope for the everything. Work for everything. Expect nothing."

"Alone." Does this mean he was alone with me or felt no connection to me and therefore feels alone despite my presence?

"Self is gone." What does this mean? Does it mean that he feels no self, no identity?

Brenan says that Ralphie can teach me. But I want more than that. I want him to get better!

I did not say "cured." I said "better." And yet this is probably a ridiculous expectation. So far we don't even know who he is, what happened to him, how he got this way. But is it possible for him to improve even without our finding it all out? In fact, doesn't his coming in here represent improvement? Of course it does! There I go again.

In any case, if he is getting better it has nothing to do with me—even though coming in to see me is evidence of wanting human contact. Perhaps this is one of those psychotic reactions that runs its course and then burns itself out. This sounds too optimistic. Acute reactions are often over in a matter of months. But chronic ones—there are people who have been in this awful place for more than forty years. Ralphie has been here for about six months.

⚯

The ward and the people looked different to him. This wasn't a big change but it was there.

People, furniture, eating utensils, and even walls and doors seemed more substantial. A new solidity had entered his world. This was not a massive thing but it was there.

Perhaps it was because everything was more focused. Before, he had looked past or around everything. Now he looked at objects. Central vision became more accentuated than peripheral vision.

This also contributed to a change in his way of walking. His walking was still mostly random. There were no actual places to go or tasks to perform. But his gait was slightly yet surely smoother, more organized, and even had a goal-directed quality to it. Nobody noticed, but there was less of the robot quality. The feel of himself had changed—only a little but something else was there.

He continued to explore and also to look at faces.

There were all kinds of faces—enraged, flat and dead, angelic, old, young, tortured, dreamy. The words "mood faces" popped into his head. The link between these words and the faces he saw gave him a sense of connection. But then he looked at a face that made his heart race. He felt his own face, which turned brick red and hot. The face looked like Frank Wilson. It was attached by a thin neck to a man who sat against a wall in a corridor off the day room. In that moment he froze. He tried to move but nothing happened. He felt his heart beat very fast. This was an intensely alive feeling and this mobilized him enough to scream within his own mind for Self. There was no response. But he moved his legs. He could walk after all. Then he realized that the man who looked like the Angel of Light ignored him and just sat in his own stuporous world staring ahead and beyond him with dead eyes.

"He is not the Angel of Light!" the voice boomed. "Who is the fool?" the voice boomed on. "You are the fool," it screamed! "You called me a fool!—yes, on the bus—'fool,' you said; 'fool, eat' you said—but you are the fool!"

Creature held his ears. He ran through the day room. Those that could got out of his way. Others got pushed aside. He could neither escape nor shut out the voice. But even as his pain continued—victimized as he was by a repetitious, mocking, screaming, "fool, fool, fool"—he realized that he was fully mobile. He also realized that Self seemed to know everything that happened to him—everything he saw or heard. Yes, everything seemed to filter through him to Self even when Self was far away. And then the voice was gone and he thought of her voice, and he slowed down to a walk. He had run. He had actually run. He had not run like that in a long time. He had no memory of his berserk flight during his "catatonic excitement" attack. The man was not the Angel of Light. His heart slowed down. Self and Self's voice were gone, but Creature realized that nothing escaped Self and that Self seemed to remember everything.

Creature took Self on many rides around the space permitted him.

Being aware that the Angel of Light was nowhere to be seen gave him a feeling of lightness.

Though his walk had changed slightly since his fright with the man who looked like Frank Wilson, the change was mostly his own illusion. There were several times when he felt that he was jumping from place to place as if he was on multiple trampolines. He felt as though he was almost flying.

Actually, something in him had shifted. The inner lifting of his mood produced the physical lightness that he felt.

This mood and the feelings that it brought to his muscles occupied him so totally that movement and exploration pushed aside all other interests. These included food and Dr. Izzabella. He forgot about both, and at one point an attendant had to cajole him to sit down and eat.

When he did he felt his arms were also lighter and easier in the work they did to lift the food to his mouth.

A change *was* taking place. Rigidity was giving way to increasing flexibility. This change was taking place in his muscles and tendons and was probably largely due to the discharge of energy which took place during his "berserk excitement." No longer having to hold so much explosive emotional energy in place, the tone of his muscles was going through a process of reduction. Ever so slowly but surely, relaxation of his muscles was replacing high tension and rigidity. Feeling free of the fear of running into the Angel of Light aided the process.

Contracture had kept arms and legs, hands and feet, neck and head pulled to the center of his body. It took great effort to pull them away from the center and to move. Relaxation allowed his limbs and his head to move from the center with greater ease and freedom. This gave him the illusion of leaping and even flying. But neither Self nor Creature were at all aware of the origin or mechanics leading to the illusion.

No one," Creature said to her.

"No one?" she asked.

"Self."

She took the chance—trying to advance her understanding even as she reassured him.

"You are someone," she said. "You have a self." He said nothing.

"You are yourself," she said. He said nothing.

She remembered what Brenan had said: "The best interpretation is one that stimulates associations—that opens up—that frees the flow of feelings and thoughts. The worst are ones that cause a closure—however correct or brilliant they may be."

I've caused a closure, she thought; and she felt discouraged.

She knew it was best to say nothing until she had a good idea where she was going.

After fifteen minutes he spoke.

"Can't follow self," he said.

This time she remained silent and only let her eyes tell him that she was listening intently.

But he said nothing.

He wanted to talk. But nothing came, and the words he needed to tell her about Self just weren't there. He could talk to Self without talking. But to talk to her or to anyone he needed the words, nearly all of which Self seemed to own.

He needed to steal them from Self or to steal Self himself and bring him to her.

He led them into deeper water.

How had he become so wise in these things? It didn't really matter. He knew. They all knew. He had attained wisdom—a special wisdom connected to sustaining life. So they were happy to swim with him into deep, clean, clear water where sight and sound were harmonious and serenely comfortable.

But then a strange thing happened. Several of them started to swim away. He called out to them but they ignored him. He realized that their course was taking them toward the coves near the shore.

He was terrified for them. He whistled loudly as only whales can in their deep fellowship—but somehow they couldn't hear or ignored what they heard. Then he realized that others were following them, and the pain he felt was intolerable.

And he found himself in the snug library talking to Thomas about time and generations.

Thomas talked about centuries and generations of ants and the many years it took to arrive at the civilized state they were in. Tim knew that all the centuries Thomas spoke of—the thousands of ant years—were only a flash—perhaps one year in the lives of other species of the universe. And the feeling of how transient and finite and small their existence was made him feel vulnerable, anxious, and sad. He had the terrible thought of how loved ones could in a flash be gone—gone from one's life forever—and could never be brought back. Then he thought of his own ending and the terrible black hole vacuum of eternity engulfed him and he ran back to the rolled up ball at the base of Creature's spine. He would rest there. Let Creature meander about. He would be as nothing at all. But even as he had those thoughts he knew that his rest could continue only as long as Creature stayed away from her.

But then he became annoyed with Creature's bouncing. It got in the way of his nothingness and he attempted to do something new. He made his dense little self heavy. He would pull against Creature's lightness. He liked Creature's sluggishness more. Creature was less human as a "slug"—a robot and not in charge. So he made the ball heavy and still heavier. But nothing happened. Creature remained light—and smooth in his movement and in his jarring bounces.

Dr. Izzabella decided to visit him—to see if she could walk with him. This was not a casual decision. She struggled with it for some time. But the temptation was powerful. She was aware of the possibility that he might have great potential for feeling painfully and dangerously coerced. Her idea was based on a twofold motive.

One—she wanted to demonstrate to him her interest.

Two—she thought that walking with him might aid in mobilizing him verbally as well as physically. She had known a catatonic patient who spoke only when he was strongly encouraged and even forced to move about physically. She thought of waiting until he came to her office to invite him to walk (as yet they had no fixed schedule or formal "sessions"). But this would defeat her first purpose. She felt that it was important to show her motivation—something of her considerable interest. Besides— four days had past and as yet he had not returned. She wanted their relationship to be sustained, and was afraid of too big a hiatus at this point. She did admit that her rationale was in part a function of her growing impatience. What made him tick was of great curiosity to her. That same curiosity about people and who they really are was, she thought, a major reason for her getting into psychiatry in the first place.

But through her own sessions with Nat Harris she knew several other things, too. She had known for a long time—perhaps always—that as with so many other people in the field, her interest was motivated by the need for self-discovery. Izz knew that joy was never an easy attainment for her.

For her entire thirty-five years she had to fight through considerable shyness, frequent sadness—though not quite depression—and what she came to think of as "pathological seriousness." In fact, Izz envied some people their superficiality and shallowness and their seemingly easy ability to generate and have fun. Her "fun" had largely been confined to scholastic achievement and to work satisfactions, though she had sustained a few relatively successful social and sexual liaisons. She lived with a man currently, also a young psychiatrist. But here too "fun" somehow eluded her. Her relationship was more comfortable than exciting. She knew that people liked her. She knew that she was very attractive—even sexy looking. She knew that she was bright. But satisfactions from these attributes meant little to her. She felt that they were only a matter of "luck." Despite herself, achievement—now in the form of helping patients—was still the area she trusted most for sustaining self-esteem.

She also knew that of late she had dreams involving her brother Pete several times a week. In her own sessions the possibility arose that she was trying to resurrect Pete through helping in the rescue and rebirth of Ralphie. But Pete knew how to have fun. He made them happy—she and her parents. He had enormous vitality. He was a presence—a joyous force. He was her only sibling. He was their only son. She knew about the guilt too—about the Freudian dynamic—of being victorious in getting rid of her younger and beloved rival for family child exclusivity. After Pete's accident they were all depressed—her parents severely—but she helped herself by helping them. Though she was still in college, she was already the therapist.

She knew, of course, that Ralphie was the antithesis of Pete. And yet who could tell what Ralphie was like or could be like. Dr. Brenan suggested that Ralphie could be a reminder of herself. If she could bring joy to him, she could bring joy to herself, and then they could perhaps both be more like Pete in this connection.

———

Come with me," she said.

He followed her to two empty, old, upholstered chairs in a corner of the day room.

"I wanted to visit you."

How could he tell her to keep talking. It was her voice that touched him. Perhaps it could touch Self, too.

But she waited for him and he lacked words.

He stared at her and she thought, My God—I feel self-conscious. It suddenly struck her that the whole psychotherapy process was an artificial contrivance and she felt angry at the institute, Freud, Horney, Brenan, all of them and all of it. She had to hold herself back from doing the human thing—to hold him, comfort him, stroke his head—something just plain warm. Couldn't a patient—better yet a person—need that—more than this formalized process of teasing out associations and making interpretations? She thought of Sandor Forenzi. Wasn't he the one who took very sick people on his lap? Was this Pete again? Had she been cold and indifferent as a sister? Why hadn't any of them taken his depression seriously? Was the accident really suicide?

Who was the patient after all? *They both were,* she thought. "All people are patients—some with a little training," Brenan said.

Gratefully, Ralphie's sudden struggle to speak interrupted these painful ruminations.

"Self," he said again and then the "no self."

On impulse she put aside analytic protocol and curiosity, too. "Let's go eat!" she said. "It's time for lunch." She led him to her office and he readily followed. She took the thermos and bag of sandwiches from the desk drawer.

He sat on one side of the desk, she on the other. She filled two paper cups with coffee.

As they ate the sandwiches, tears rolled down his cheeks. She noticed immediately but said nothing. She also noted with satisfaction that his appetite was very good.

"Self is crying," he said. This, without questions or comment on her part, surprised her and she said nothing. They went on eating even though his tears continued. She felt good. More than good. She felt free, lose, relaxed. *Am I experiencing a loosening in him?* she thought. *No, I just feel free, somehow,* she answered. Then she theorized that it came from dropping the "therapeutic discipline." She felt that eating together may have greater therapeutic value than any brilliant interpretation she could give him. In any case, it was highly therapeutic to herself, she thought. But then the thoughts of eating with Pete and her parents made her sad.

But she still felt good.

"He's crying," said Creature.

"He?" she asked.

"He's crying," Creature repeated flatly.

"You mean to say, '*I'm* crying.' " *He, self, alienation and detachment*, she thought.

"*He!*" Creature said, this time with a slight rise in affect which she noted as significant. Now she wasn't at all sure that his use of the words "he" and "self" to talk about himself was a function of detachment.

"Who is 'he'?" she asked very gently.

Creature did not respond. She said nothing. They finished the sandwiches. Izz felt and looked relaxed. Creature was stiff, but more relaxed than he had been since he began his trip to the bridge.

"Not me!" he answered.

And then she got goose flesh. It occurred to her that he was talking about somebody else. She no longer felt relaxed. Queasiness replaced well-being. Could he be a multiple? she asked herself. Could he be both a multiple and schizophrenic?

But he said nothing else. In fact he got up, left her, and walked to the day room. She did nothing to stop him and did not follow him.

Dr. Izzabella's Notes

How could he be a multiple personality? Multiple personality is a neurotic condition. Ralphie is blatantly psychotic. His diagnosis is obvious. The rigidity; his autism—even complete stupor—his acting-out excitement. Everything here substantiates catatonic schizophrenia. Dr. Brenan says diagnostic categories are not to be taken too seriously. He says to remember that every human being is different, including those with "identical diagnostic labels."

Several people I spoke to on the child and adolescent unit said that in adolescence much symptomatic overlapping is possible. This is especially so in acute reactions.

Is Ralphie's schizophrenia acute or has he been psychotic all of his life? Is he a true multiple or is this some kind of acute, short-lived reaction? Is he a multiple at all? If he is—who is Self?

I like the term "Self." Does this mean he still has a self, some kind of integrated identity some place in him. Nat Harris says everyone has a self! Some of the people here are more like automatons than selves and yet perhaps Harris is right. As for diagnostic categories—why should they hold up? Why should we expect consistency? Human beings are, after all, capable of just about any and all combinations and permutations of behavior and unpredictability.

Am I wise to abandon psychotherapeutic discipline? Lunch and my spontaneity today seemed productive. Perhaps he needs me as a person—yes, even a mothering person more than me in any kind of professional stance. Isn't this a form of love—the kind of therapy Forenzi and Otto Rank spoke of and that Horney called human support?

Of course too much closeness can come over as a threat. Nat Harris warned me that some patients need and demand to sit on your lap and to be hugged and loved and once on your lap they scratch your eyes out. But Ralphie certainly maintains his distance.

I wonder if he likes ice cream.

———————

It was the first time he saw the television set in the day room. The winter sun shined on its blank screen through the window giving the illusion that the set was on. First he saw little ants scurrying about doing their work, very busy but stopping now and then to talk to one another. There was something odd about these ants that was conveyed to him, something familiar. He was not aware, but it was their humanity. Then the ants faded, and just as though the channel was changed a whole new scene appeared. It was the open sea—deep water, and there just beneath the surface a group of huge, powerful, and majestic whales swam along gracefully. They, too, conveyed a human quality, again providing a familiar feeling to him. This was almost, but not quite, a déjà vu experience.

Suddenly he had the urge to run away and he ran through the day room back to the ward and his bed. People remembering his "berserk run" days earlier quickly got out of his way. But he could not forget the T.V. set and he finally went back to the day room, approaching the T.V. very slowly.

For several minutes there was nothing on the screen. Then it turned black, and after a few minutes it turned brilliant white, and then images came into focus. As the images sharpened, the white glare disappeared; then the screen and the T.V. set itself vanished, leaving only the scene hanging in mid air. He saw the ants and the whales kaleidoscope together, filling the scene. Then he saw an image, poorly defined at first, rise up from the lower right corner of the scene. Then the same thing took place in the upper left corner of the scene. The two images merged in the center of the kaleidoscoped whales and ants and, as one, immediately became clear. In that moment he saw Self. He recognized his own face. He let out a muffled, anguished scream and as he did he knew where Self went when he was away. The scene vanished. The television set turned off, was there on again. He was exhausted; it seemed like a very long walk to his bed.

———————

In the dream she took his hand and they walked. They said nothing, but they both knew they were looking for Self. As she started to lead him to her office he pulled back and led her. She willingly followed. He took her to the day room and then they stood still. He couldn't move. He was paralyzed by Self. With great effort he let go of her hand, and with even greater effort he managed say, "T.V." She did not respond. "T.V," he said again, and getting these words out exhausted him. She looked at the T.V.—the screen was blank. She continued to stare at the blank T.V. but nothing happened.

When she turned from it he pleaded with her not to give up— to keep looking—to see Self, ants, and whales. But she couldn't hear him because his pleas were only in his mind. He couldn't move his mouth to convey them to her.

Then he looked at the screen. No ants! No whales! Only Self grinning—his own face grinning and superimposed over buildings exploding, torrents of blood running, skys falling, mountains trembling, winds howling, masses of people killing, dying, and screaming, airplanes falling and burning cars colliding, ships sinking, people drowning, and the face—the superimposed face of Self—laughing hysterically. He was seeing the end of the world.

But she saw none of it. She just walked serenely out of the day room.

When he woke he continued to picture the T.V. set and saw little else in his mind's eye or anywhere else for the rest of the day.

In her dream Ralphie said, "Izzy be my family."

"I'm your doctor," she said.

"Don't leave me," he said.

When she was about to answer he turned to the wall and then back to her. But he wasn't Ralphie at all. He was a stranger. Then when he said, "We are family," she realized it was her brother Pete, ten years older than when he died.

In the dream she wept and then laughed.

When she woke she ached with disappointment, but the thought that he needed kinship more than therapy stayed with her. Is this what we all need? she asked herself. For several hours she could not shake her intense feelings of loneliness.

Dr. Izzabella's Notes:

I brought him ice cream and we both ate it. He seemed to like it, but he still seemed subdued and somewhat rigid. I guess I expected some kind of ice-cream breakthrough. He didn't even finish his first portion. Of course, that didn't stop me. I remember how Pete and I used to go at it.

When he got up to leave of his own accord I followed along. I had the impression that this was what he wanted.

He led me to the T.V. set and just stood there and stared at it. What kinds of visions was he seeing? Visual hallucinations? Imaginary fantasies? Nothing at all?

I turned on the set and I had the feeling that he didn't see or hear it. I changed channels and this had no effect. I raised the volume and he didn't seem to notice. It was as if he saw something beyond the images on the screen. He was riveted, and I wonder if this isn't part of the catatonic process.

I finally said good-bye and walked away. He didn't notice at all.

What about my dream? I miss Pete! I want us to be a family! I don't like being an only child! Child? Thirty-five—some child! Did I really want to be an only child? Was there any aspect of Pete's death that I wanted? Horrendous thought—but possible, of course. In any case, he is not Pete and my work must not become a substitute family. I must keep things separated. Can feelings be kept separate?

But if the dream is a message to myself, what am I trying to tell myself?

That I miss Pete—I know that.

That Ralphie needs a friend—family—closeness? Perhaps. But at the T.V. set he was in his own world—almost autistic, removed—awake but gone. I feel certain that he didn't see the stuff on the screen, but I'll bet anything there was something there that held him. *Something?* Some inner-world projection. Perhaps I should have asked him what he saw. It occurred to me—but I hold back. It may be better that way—to wait until he's ready—to respect his reserve, his being closed. Words from outside himself may be felt as dynamite to him. But maybe this is too melodramatic. In any case, I don't want to be too cool, too reserved with him. I want to continue the ambiance of spontaneity I have felt lately with him. I have to guard against getting into a highly controlled analytic mode. I don't think I'd ever reach him with that. On the other hand, I don't want to be intrusive enough to inundate him. I feel that it would take very little to close him off and to lose him. But I do feel very strongly that he needs *me* the person more than any analytic interpretations I could give him. I hope this is not too colored by obvious counter-transference.

⟨⟨⟩⟩

Izz and Ralphie played Ping-Pong.

She led him to the adolescent unit where several tables were located. He was oblivious to the fact that he was among people close to his own age. While he complied with her directions, he seemed utterly distracted.

This was not an ordinary game of Ping-Pong because of his lack of any application to the game. Indeed, she decided that he just wasn't there. He seemed even to be in more of a haze than usual. She wondered if he was slipping back into a catatonic stupor. Was she moving too fast? Threatening him with activities beyond his current abilities? Too much socialization? But she decided to continue.

She put a racket in his hand and placed him at one end of the table. He complied easily but did not cooperate. She served the ball to him. He did nothing.

An attendant stood behind him and threw the ball back at her, and for twenty minutes this non-game of Ping-Pong went on.

And then a change took place.

He became focused on the ball and on her. He didn't exactly play, but he moved the racket so that the ball hit it every few shots. He was clearly out of his haze. He had returned from wherever he had been. She spoke to him encouragingly without pushing or even prompting.

She had the feeling that she had stirred something from the past. Perhaps he had played Ping-Pong before, or maybe it was the playfulness, the simple humanity of the thing. In any case, even though he missed the balls and it was the attendant who returned them, he seemed more alive—more *with it*. Perhaps she could get him to really play one day soon.

But then after only ten minutes of relatively "being with it" he seemed tired, and she led him back to the day room. He had not returned the ball—not even once—but she had the feeling that it had been a constructive experience.

—◄▥▥◙▥▥►—

The truck moved down the street until it came to the little white house with the green shutters.

There was all kinds of furniture and cartons and the last thing they took out of the truck was the enormous rubber plant in the big butter tub. The woman told the men to be very careful with it, and she never took her eyes off them as they brought it into the house. Then they took an aquarium into the house. It was a fifty- or sixty-gallon tank almost completely full of water. It was beautifully set up and looked as if a piece of ocean, with fish and plants, had been transported to this place. The men were very careful with it and not a drop of water was lost. A boy stood by and watched their every move much as the woman had done with the potted rubber plant.

He had no curiosity about the woman or the boy. He was conscious of their presence but never looked at their faces. His total concentration was on the plant and the aquarium.

Before they placed any of the furniture, the woman directed the men to place the plant in front of a window, and the boy had the tank placed on the adjacent wall.

Then the people were gone. Then the house was gone. Only the rubber plant remained, and the pot and the plant grew until they filled the entire space. Then the tub was gone. Only the anthill remained, and the ants scurried about doing their business.

As Creature looked on an intense feeling of loneliness filled him—it was a feeling but it gave him no satisfaction. With no ability to identify it, it was nevertheless very powerful. He wanted a connection. He wanted to be part of something—not just something—a community. He wanted to be one of something—to feel himself as a contributing someone to others who together formed a something. So, as he watched, he wanted to be one of them. He wanted what Self had been able to have. He wanted—he needed—to enter the anthill. He tried. It was no use. It was too small and he was too big. The ants seemed very happy. But he remained the outsider looking in.

Then a transformation took place. Sound—a full, rich sound growing in complexity and volume—filled the place and swept the anthill away, leaving a great undersea scene. But the aquarium fish were no longer there. They had all turned into whales—and all kinds were represented. There were humpbacks, sperm, blue, killer, right whales, and more. They were all there, and then there was the sound. It was their song. He was immersed in their sound. All else was obliterated. Within minutes he entered a euphoric haze. He and the symphonic sound had become a unity devoid of tension of any kind. Then the water was gone and so were the whales. Consciousness of himself had evaporated, too. He had become the sound, and nothing else existed or mattered; but there was a moment—perhaps only a second or two—in which he identified with Self and his voyages. Time, space, and even existence were obliterated. He had no idea or memory afterward that, after many hours, someone had led him back from the T.V. set to his bed.

—◦◦◦—

Self."

"What about Self?" she asked.

"In the sound." He said this without struggle, which she noticed happily. But she also thought, *It makes no sense—he has a thought disorder.*

"Sound?"

"He's there!" he actually said this emphatically. There was more affect in these two words than anything he had said to her up to this time. *Perhaps this is not a thought disorder,* she thought, and tried to pursue it for meaning.

"Where?" she asked.

"With them." he answered without hesitation.

"Them?" She was excited but asked "them?" very gently and softly.

"Ants and whales," he said.

This made no sense to her at all, and again she thought of word salads and schizophrenic gibberish characteristic of some thought disorders.

"The sound," he volunteered.

"Sound?" she asked.

"Self is there," he answered.

"Bring him here," she said on a hunch.

"He won't come," he answered.

"Tell him he must," she commanded—she said this as gently as a command could be and still be a command.

Creature said nothing. Then he began to visibly stiffen. She was afraid she had gone too far.

"Let's play Ping-Pong," she suggested.

To her surprise he was not stiff at the table. She still needed the attendant to back him up, although he did have the racket in position so that the ball hit it a few times. She thought he might even be concentrating on the game but then felt this was only wish-fulfilling on her part.

She tried to talk to him while they played—wary all the time of pushing him into catatonic stiffness.

"Self," she stated.

This got his attention and now the racket was at his side and she hit the ball back and forth to the attendant. But although he stared at her he said nothing.

"I would so much like to see him," she implored.

"Why?"

The answer startled her. First, this was actually direct and meaningful dialogue. But more than that, the word was said in a voice and manner she had not heard before. It was strong, deep, and had a definite imperious quality.

"Because I want to help him," she said, and now she was

convinced that somebody was there besides Ralphie. But he remained silent.

As they walked back to his ward she tried to engage him in conversation again.

"The sound?" she enquired.

He tried to say something but it was the same as at his earliest. Though there seemed to be words, he couldn't get them out. His face was contorted with effort as if to get past an invisible inhibiting force.

She was tempted to push him—to go on, to break through. But she decided against it, and by the time they got back they were both silent.

Dr. Izzabella's Notes:

He is not alone! That "why?" was not *his* voice! Someone else is there! Self? Is he a multiple? Catatonic? Catatonic with multiple personality? And of what importance is it to categorize clinically? Beran says clinical diagnosis has some descriptive value but can have a destructive effect therapeutically. It can lead to constriction—to pushing the patient into one or another diagnostic category even though they refuse to quite fit. It also destroys individuality—we start to see all "schizophrenics" as one and the same person: actually each and every one is different and there are any number of subtle combinations and permutations. Is this all some kind of defense of Ralphie—of my particular interest in him? Countertransference again? Pete again? What difference? Ralphie is what he is. But Self?—Who is Self and how do I find out?

If there is splitting here—and a catatonic reaction as well—an acute autistic reaction—what kind of brutality produced it? There was no evidence of physical abuse on admission here or on record from Bellvue. Who is Ralphie, anyway?—Who is Self? Who is this boy? What is he—other than a very pained, hurt, frightened boy? More important, what can I do for him? Am I wrong to withhold an Amytal interview—narco hypnosis? I think not; at least not at this point, because he seems to be opening up and getting closer to me. But now more than ever I

must be careful not to inadvertently close the door—maybe forever. I think of our chronic wards—people locked up in themselves—forty and more years of autism.

Amazing what I've come to think of as "opening up"—but
every human being has her or his own frame of reference. I must
also keep in mind that a timetable is an individual matter, and
not attempt to rush.

But I also have the persistent feeling that passivity and professional detachment are the least things Ralphie needs!

I must not neglect my other patients. Yet there is so little I
can do for them—maintenance. Ralphie is my only real therapy
case here. But let's face it, is it more than interest or even hope
or even Pete? I like him. I care. I just do. Perhaps if this gets
through to him it will have an effect—a good one, I hope—
something to neutralize what must be terrible self-hate and rage.

<hr />

He had to get in. But he was a thousand times too large. No—
perhaps a million times too large. He had to bring himself down
to their size. But he couldn't. He simply was not one of them.
He could not become part of their schema. He no longer had
the ability. He was blocked. He was desperate. Creature must be
destroyed! It was his fault! And then he couldn't even see them
clearly. They were too small. William, Tina, Louise—they went
into their ant house and he couldn't see them.

And then he couldn't swim! And he couldn't find them. He
was much too small and the oceans were too big. He listened
intently—more than intently, intensely—so intensely that it
hurt—but he couldn't hear their sound. There was only silence.

And he heard tinkles. It was her voice and it said, "Come out,
come out, wherever you are."

<hr />

He watched the T.V. screen intently. He would use this way to go back. He would create those worlds and he would step in and this time he would never come back.

And then it was there, on the screen, all of it was there. Strangely, Creature was there also. But he could not enter. All his effort was to no avail. Each time he attempted to enter the scene, he heard her voice: "Come out, come out wherever you are." He tried to ignore her, to blot out the words, but the effort to enter the scene made her voice louder and her words clearer.

In desperation, since he couldn't enter the scene, he tried to blot it out. But this, too, was to no avail. It persisted despite his struggle to obliterate it. He decided to run from it all—back to his bed—but now her voice said, "Stay." It was very gentle. This word, "stay"—gentle and soft. It paralyzed him. He couldn't even turn around. But suddenly the screen went blank. Voices and sound—her sound—were gone. He could not go back, but at least he had succeeded in part. He still had some control, he thought.

And then it was there again—all of it on the screen—the voices of Tim, Tina, William, Louise; the whale song and her voice—"Come out, come out, wherever you are," she said. He tried to shut her out, to shut all of it out, but his struggle had no effect at all. He screamed but nobody heard a thing. It was a scream without voice. He would close his eyes. He would squeeze them shut, tight. But it didn't help. It was all there. He could see all of it through his eyelids and he could not close his ears. Her voice sang to the whale sound—"You must come out now, you must come out."

Creature moved stiffly and slowly to the center of the screen and the whales and ants and Creature kaleidoscoped together. And then for a moment they separated. Creature looked very sad and his eyes seemed to be pleading but he had no voice. Then the whales, singing their beautiful symphony, glided into a part of the sea that seemed to be boiling. Their song stopped. All was silence. They swam into shallow coves. Shots rang out. And there was the plant—the earth was dry. The leaves were falling. The ants were dying and the plant was being moved—to be thrown away. He was in anguish but could do nothing. Her voice said, "Come out" and the scene exploded and the screen went blank. Then a ball began to form in the center of the screen. At first it was vague, translucent, little more than a shadow. But it soon took on substance and filled the entire screen. Next it became concentrated center-screen. It then uncurled, unraveled, became linear, vertical, and walked smoothly out of the set.

He continued to stare at the screen but now it had turned black. Sorrow filled him. He collapsed on the floor, writhing in anguish. They put him to bed and sedated him. He soon fell into a deep, dreamless sleep.

IV

Can you help me go back?"

This was not Ralphie!

"They need me. I need them."

This voice, the pronunciation—it was older, cultivated. There was no hesitation—no difficulty at all getting words out. It simply wasn't Ralphie.

Trying to be calm, or at least sound calm, she asked the question very gently.

"They? Who are they? What are their names? Your name?"

"Tim, William, Tina, Louise, George, and the others," he said at once—his voice and manner eager now.

Where is Ralphie? she thought. And then before she could hold it back she said it.

"Where is he?"

"Where is Ralphie?"

She felt she had made a mistake. She should have asked who Tim, Tina, and the others were. But for the moment it was too late.

"Ralphie?"

She had to go on now.

"Yes, the boy who was here."

"Ralphie?"

"Yes!"

"Why do you call him Ralphie?"

She was startled and stymied. First, because she had no answer; secondly, because the question and manner of asking were so completely natural. This simply was not the same person she had been dealing with—if he was a patient at all. But she knew better, and she regained self-control and was once again doctor and therapist. He certainly looked the same—

that is, he was the same person as before and that was reassuring. But in fact he did not look the same. Yes, his features, body, and so on were the same. But expression, movement, impression had no connection to Ralphie. The catatonic overlay was not there. He seemed older. More than that, he projected a relatively in-charge-of-self feeling. But his next words belied that impression.

"Help me back," he pleaded. "Please." She said nothing.

"You brought me here," he said flatly. She said nothing.

"You told him to bring me."

"Him?"

"Creature."

"Creature?"

Now she knew. Creature was Ralphie.

"They are gone—all gone—even Creature—he's gone, too." She found no words.

"I'm alone," he said flatly, as if stating a fact to himself.

"I'm here," she said, and she felt utterly helpless.

"I'm here for you," she added and felt that her words were flat, inappropriate, and foolish.

"You remind me of someone."

"Who?" she asked—barely believing that an actual dialogue was taking place.

"I don't know." She thought he sounded hopeless—hopeless and helpless, she thought.

And then it ended. Their conversation was over. He got up and walked out.

—◁≡◎≡▷—

It was as if he was seeing the ward for the first time. He knew his way around, but it still felt new and also gray and shoddy. This accentuated his terrible longing for the other places and for them—Tina, George, and the rest. But he knew it. There was no going back.

And Creature. What had happened to Creature? He knew the

answer even as he asked it, and it filled him with self-loathing. He had become Creature. They were one and the same. The simple, no-needing Self was gone. The safe, detached, protected Self was gone. The merger was complete, and with it came vulnerability and intense self-hate.

He looked at his arms and hands and legs and feet and fingers and they all seemed strange and disconnected and frightening. He was trapped in an alien body of fragments. He was that alien body and he found himself to be in an alien, gray, souless, terrible place, and he screamed.

He stood in the middle of the day room and screamed in anguish and his voice sounded distant and removed, too, and the feel of it was made even stranger by the lack of response from the many other disconnected people floating and dragging around. But it was more than that. The scream was not a release. It felt removed, disconnected, and incomplete and futile. It was as if there was a large mass of feeling about to burst and the scream, if it were only hooked to it, could scream it out. But it was not hooked. The feelings remained intact and the scream remained disconnected from them—a product of anguish, but telling only a fragment—a tiny fragment of what he felt.

And despite his pain and terror he said to Creature:

"Are you satisfied—are you satisfied now?" But there was no answer and he knew there would be no answer because there was no Creature. There was only himself and he was Creature, and questions and answers came from and went back to the same source and were really a monologue and not a dialogue at all.

Dr. Izabella's Notes:

I'm dumbfounded, shocked, frightened, fascinated, and grateful. I'm also deeply confused. But what do we have here? Let me marshall my impressions.

1) He seems older—perhaps seventeen, even eighteen.
2) He is intelligent and cultivated. This is definitely an impression—no hard evidence, but the way he articulates his words is significant.
3) He is very sad.

4) He wants to go back! To what—his catatonic state? To some disassociative fantasy life? To where he was before he came here?

5) The change in him is radical, acute, frightening. It has a Dr. Jekyll/Mr. Hyde quality in its complete contrast. Is this part of the disassociative, multiple personality process or is it simply coming out of the catatonic, sluggish state of acute psychosis—or both?

6) "You brought me here." I brought him where? To the hospital? To his current state of awareness—from out of contact to in contact? To a severe state of current inner conflict and anxiety?

7) How did I bring him wherever I brought him? Transference? From whom is he transferring what to me? If my effect alone can "bring him back," so to speak—I surely connect him to people he knows. This also means that I can easily push him back to being out of contact again—or can I?

8) Who are Tim, George, Tina, William? Creature brought him. Disassociation? Multiple?

9) How to proceed? With great care. But I believe it was spontaneity—lunch, Ping-Pong—that did it. I must combine care and spontaneity. I must guard against becoming professionally wooden. The line is narrow—very narrow.

The surprise is fascinating, but also makes me very anxious. Who is he? Did I like him more as sluggish, stuttering Ralphie? More predictable? Manageable? I don't know. I'm still shocked. I was getting to know little Ralphie. I don't know *Him.* Who are Tim, George, Tina?

I'm afraid."

"Of what?"

"I will blow apart. Explode." This, she noted, was said almost without affect; but she took his words with utmost seriousness.

"I felt nothing—nothing. I feel too much now. It's all here,

inside." He pointed to his chest. But it was all said in a flat tone—
almost without affect. The thought that he seemed the antithesis
of explosive occurred to her.

"Tell me—tell me what you feel."

"I'll blow up. I'll come apart."

"Can you let it come out slowly?" She asked this most gently.

"You don't understand." He was dejected now. This was
much more appropriate than the flatness.

They said nothing for ten minutes.

"Who are the people you want to go back to?"

"People?"

"Tina, Tim, George, William?"

"You don't understand."

"Help me to understand."

He stared off into space and she wondered where he was.

"What are you thinking about?"

"Nothing."

"What do you see?"

"The world is a potted rubber plant."

She smiled, but he did not respond to her smile and stared off
again.

"How is it a rubber plant?" she asked.

"All the oceans connect," he responded, and she quickly
thought, He has a thought disorder and is very sick.

"What shall I call you?" she asked.

"I don't know."

"Ralphie?"

"No!"

"What did they call you?"

"Tim, George."

"Then your name is Tim, George."

"No." he said.

"Tim and George are other people?"

"No!" and this time there was slight affect in his voice.

They sat silently for at least ten minutes. She felt that she was
prying and that he was annoyed. Perhaps she was going too
quickly.

"Call me 'Self,' " he said, and he walked out.

Dr. Izzabella's Notes:

His affect is inappropriate relative to the explosive feelings he describes.

Considering his catatonic reaction, the main feeling he is holding down must be anger. No! It has to be rage. It takes incredible rage to produce the rigidity of catatonia. His catatonic excitement certainly evidenced his rage in action.

How do I tap this anger, free him from his paralysis, and not precipitate a total regression—a catatonic stupor?

He is now in contact and I'm as in the dark as ever. Contact—relatively in contact at best—at least not stuporous, but nothing that resembles real communication.

Am I afraid of his potential for explosions?

Is he dangerous?

Sedation?

He is hardly what I'd call lively now—sedation would slow him up still more. That would be counterproductive. I *am afraid*. Both Brenan and Harris tell me I must be careful. How can I be careful and not let my fear get in the way of his progress? I saw what he could do when he explodes. I like him. Does he know that? Am I being an emotional fool—a love-solves-all idiot? I have no answers. Strange how I am afraid now when he seems to be getting better, and yet I know that Brenan and Harris are right. There could be danger here. I have no answers. There are no answers. What strange work this is. Groping in the dark? Am I being melodramatic? Feeling heroic? Self-idealizing? Enough about me! What about him? I care. I care about everyone here! But I do care more about him—some doctor—but it's true—none of which is helpful—but maybe it is—maybe he realized this and that's why he "came back"—or "out" or whatever—because he is in fact my favorite patient. Sounds awful. Maybe there's no danger here at all—I don't know. I just don't know. But I'll go slowly. I won't prod. I'll listen. I must remember this is not any kind of conventional psychoanalysis with an outpatient. This is a very sick, hospitalized boy.

Then it happened. In the day room. The abcess was lanced.

Frank Wilson, the Angel of Light, had returned.

He was suddenly there facing Self. He started to talk, as if to apologize.

The dam broke! Self screamed and the pus of rage exploded out of him.

Frank Wilson fled as soon as the outburst began. Everyone ran. He was alone in the day room. But this time there was no further physical acting out. Indeed, he stood in one place, hands at his sides, screaming.

His entire being—all energy—was dedicated to the scream. At first it was a long, long scream, wordless—just a terrible high-pitched sound that went on and on, interrupted by guttural choking sounds with each intake of air. Then, after at least ten minutes, there were words that seemed to tear out of his throat. They were rasping and harsh and also unintelligible, they were a stream of associations and memories related to the past, both distant and close. Then there was sobbing and more screaming without words and then with words, and his face was wet with mucous and tears. No one knew it, but in the last minutes of the explosion deep, gut-wrenching sadness had replaced anger. The words that were unintelligible told of his terrible longing for Louise, William, Tina, George, and the others.

She saw and heard it all from the doorway and prevented the attendants and nurses from interrupting.

The entire episode lasted some twenty minutes, and then he was suddenly silent and walked slowly to his bed.

He slept for eighteen hours and did not dream. She left orders for him not to be disturbed.

V

Feel better?" This was said after a very long silence.

"I feel."

"What do you feel?"

"Small, very small," and then as an afterthought, "Creature is big."

"Creature?"

"The body person."

"And the non-body person?" This asked as a hunch because she felt she was groping.

"I, Self, am the non-body person."

"But you have a body. Your body is here. Your body brought you here." I am saying too much, she thought.

"Yes. He brought me here."

His responses up to this point were relatively flat—cooperative but significantly toneless or monotone—no feeling—no fluctuation of speech or mood. She thought of schizophrenic flattened affect. She also wondered about his disassociation from his body. Was he a multiple personality? Was this part of a depersonalization schizophrenic process? Drop the clinical stuff, she told herself, and then she remembered that he had said he did feel, that he felt small.

"Creature is big?"

"Bigger than I feel." This time there was affect, but it was one of sadness—a deep-down sorrow. Her own association was a picture of her brother; the word "loss" popped into her mind and she wondered what or whom it might have been that he had lost.

"But you—the body that brought you—is you."

"Yes," he said, and this was surely the saddest "yes" she had ever heard.

In the dream he argued with Creature. He told Creature to behave as a creature and he would be a self again—a ball self. Creature said, "No!" emphatically. And then he saw Creature holding Dr. Izzabella's hand and he felt that they would stand against him. But he tried again. He said, "We will be apart but together." Creature smirked. "I mean I will be there, my ball self, I will be there with you. I will not leave," and this time Izzabella said, "No!" as he saw the ocean and whales and as he saw a huge potted rubber plant and as he knew that he was lying to Creature. Then Izzabella said, "No!" again and this time her voice was so loud he woke from the dream. His urge to see her and to try to persuade her was very strong.

As he walked to her office he knew that the plant was only a plant and that the whales were only whales. The whales had no names and he realized that in the dream he saw the plant but no ants. His sense of loss felt like a solid mass in his chest, and his longing for the ant and whale families he had been part of produced a sadness that drove away all thoughts and fantasies.

I want to go back!"

"To what?" she asked, and received no answer.

"To where?" she tried.

"To when?" she tried again.

"To being two of us—Self and Creature." She said nothing.

"Can you help me?" he asked, softly.

"But you are doing much better now."

"Now I have nobody," he said very softly, so that she had to strain to hear him.

"Who did you have before?" she asked gently.

"I had William, Tina, and Louise, and when I was George instead of Tim, I could swim a thousand miles and was part of the great music they made. They were my family, too—whales, beautiful whales, and we talked to each other across a thousand miles." Then he seemed agitated, and tears streamed down his cheeks as he started to weep.

"What is upsetting you?" she asked.

"I am here. I should be there with them. I must warn them. If they go into the coves they will be shot."

They sat and said nothing.

Then he said, "It is too late. I can no longer go back and my warning would be too late now.

"And the same is true for the others."

"The others?" she asked.

"William, Tina, and Louise. The rubber plant was flooded with water and the whole colony of ants was drowned. The plant died. It was thrown away."

"How do you know?" she asked.

"I just know," he said. "I just know."

And then his weeping turned into deep sobbing.

She held his shoulders. She tried to comfort him.

"It was a dream," she said. But even as she said it she felt there was something more here than a dream—perhaps an ongoing hallucinatory fantasy—part of a delusional disassociative reaction.

He calmed down. The weeping stopped.

They sat silently. He was obviously miserable. But misery was a normal human feeling, after all, and she viewed this, too, as a step forward even as she felt terribly sorry for him.

Then on a hunch she asked, "Did your mother have a rubber plant in her house?"

He became very pale and then bolted out of the room.

She was startled by his reaction, and at first she just froze. Then she wondered if she should go after him—comfort him? Investigate further? She wanted to go to him but decided to stay and wait. This took considerable effort. Then she thought of the rubber plant and what meaning it had for him.

Feeling quite agitated, he went back to sit on his bed.

In a few minutes he calmed down and a strange memory intruded. He remembered calling himself Little Ralphie when someone at the city hospital asked him his name. But he couldn't fathom why. It must have been Creature who told them this name, he decided.

But soon the rubber plant was there again in his mind's eye. His vision was of a woman throwing away a potted rubber plant, complaining that there were ants all over it, and of a little boy weeping.

That night he slept without dreaming. It was the longest, deepest sleep he had had in many months. Again Dr. Izzabella made sure that nobody disturbed him. When he woke it was early afternoon and he felt that something deep in himself had changed. He went directly to her office. On the way a flood of things from the past drowned out all else.

                       ⚊⚊

She was amazed at his newfound affect. The flatness was gone, replaced by almost palpable feelings and animation.

"Yes, my mother had a rubber plant. For a long time I knew there was a colony of tiny ants that lived there. No one else saw them. I used to have fantasies of being one of them. My father had a huge goldfish tank. I used to pretend they were whales. I was very interested in insects and whales and read a lot about both." This was all said in a rush, as if it was urgent to get all of it to her before it vanished.

"What are their names—your family?" she asked most gently.

"My father's name was William." He smiled and went on.

"My Mother's name was Tina.

"My sister's name was Louise.

"My little brother's name was Ralphie.

"My name is Tim.

"My grandfather's name was George.

"This was my family," he said with a deep sigh. "This was my family. There was no one else."

"You say *was* for them. Where are they now?"

"They're gone," he said very quietly and repeated, "they're gone."

"Where?" she asked.

In an almost inaudible voice he told her.

"It was my birthday. We went to a beautiful restaurant. There were glass windows all around. We sat in a cove in the front— a big round table. We were happy and then it happened." He stopped.

"What happened?" she asked in a whisper.

"A car, no it was a truck. It smashed through the glass. Everyone was killed." This was said matter of factly.

But then he was suddenly racked with sobs. A great emotional dam was broken. Through the sobs he said, "Except me, except me—I wasn't even scratched. If it wasn't my birthday we never would have gone there."

"It was in no way your fault," she tried to console him.

He could hardly catch his breath between his sobs but managed to say with deep anguish—

"The screams, the crashing glass, the terrible noise and blood all over—I couldn't get it out of my mind."

She put her arms around him and hugged him tightly and whispered,

"Tim, you will soon be leaving this awful place. You've been here for almost a year."

Through his sobs he asked,

"Will I see you?"

"Yes," she said. "I'll be leaving here, too, and we will arrange it—to see each other."

"I have no one," he said, and now his crying had stopped.

"You have yourself," she said, "and me—I'll be there." She steeled herself, but her eyes filled with tears and she easily felt his and her own loneliness.

End Note

Therapists who are effective, invariably come to love their patients. This *love* has no sexual basis. It is connected to love of human beings and love of the healing process. For these doctors, nurses, social workers, psychologists, psychiatrists, and psychoanalysts, there is no greater satisfaction than relieving pain, especially emotional pain. In this way, treatment results in help for both patient and therapist.

Indeed, the privilege of participating in healthy progress in another human being's life brings more than self-satisfaction and self-help. Helping other people discover their constructive inner resources brings deep, abiding joy.

Having for many years participated in this process of aiding self-realization has been among the most joyous experiences of my life. Indeed, it has sustained me and continues to be a source of happiness and fulfillment.

T. I. R.

813
Rub

Rubin, Theodore
  Isaac.

David and Lisa.

DATE			